MURDER

—— along the ——
YELLOWSTONE TRAIL

The Execution of Seth Danner

Was he guilty?

Kelly Hartman

KELLY SUZANNE HARTMAN

*With Contributions by the Gallatin Historical Society
and Gallatin History Museum*

H
THE
History
PRESS

Published by The History Press
Charleston, SC
www.historypress.com

Front cover: author photo; *inset*: Gallatin Historical Society/Gallatin History Museum.
Back cover, top: Gallatin Historical Society/Gallatin History Museum; *bottom*: Gallatin Historical Society/Gallatin History Museum; *top inset*: courtesy Janet (Danner) Mann; *bottom inset*: Gallatin Historical Society/Gallatin History Museum.

First published 2020

Manufactured in the United States

ISBN 9781467144544

Library of Congress Control Number: 2020932097

Notice: The information in this book is true and complete to the best of our knowledge. It is offered without guarantee on the part of the author or The History Press. The author and The History Press disclaim all liability in connection with the use of this book.

Up ahead they's a thousan' lives we might live, but when it comes it'll on'y be one.
—*John Steinbeck,* The Grapes of Wrath

I have made peace with my God, and will go to him knowing that I am fully prepared.
—*Seth Danner, July 18, 1924*

CONTENTS

CONTENTS

SETH DANNER FAMILY TREE

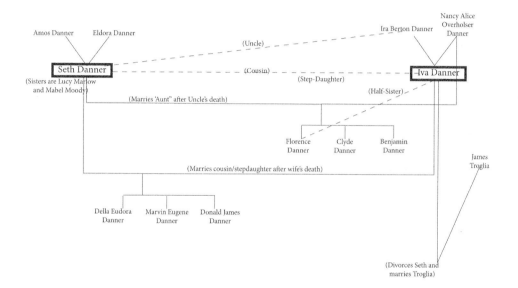

Amos Danner   Eldora Danner   Ira Berton Danner   Nancy Alice Overholser Danner

(Uncle)

Seth Danner   (Cousin)   Iva Danner

(Sisters are Lucy Marlow and Mabel Moody)   (Step-Daughter)   (Half-Sister)

(Marries 'Aunt" after Uncle's death)

Florence Danner   Clyde Danner   Benjamin Danner

(Marries cousin/stepdaughter after wife's death)

                                                          James Troglia

Della Eudora Danner   Marvin Eugene Danner   Donald James Danner

(Divorces Seth and marries Troglia)

PREFACE

While I can't say that Seth Danner is innocent, I can't say that he is guilty, either.

When I was about five years old, my family visited a museum in downtown Bozeman, Montana, to cool off on a hot day. All I remember is the brick of the building, but my dad vividly remembers the gallows located inside the building. He remembers how much it bothered him visually, but that is all he remembers. The story of the gallows was missing and had been missing until twenty-five years later, when I became curator at that same museum, the Gallatin History Museum.

To cope with having such a grim reminder of mortality to walk under every day, I decided to face that darkness to try to find a light. And I did. It's not a glimmering light of overwhelming hope or joy—no, it's a light of illumination. I can say that I understand life a little better, the extreme hardships those in our past have faced and those we still face today. I understand that human life is interesting, complicated and yet so very simple. I hope those who read this book see this paradox of qualities in the characters of Seth Danner and those who condemned him.

There are many to thank for the completion of this book, but a few in particular were invaluable to my work: Margie Kankrilik, for transcribing hundreds of newspapers articles and letters and for putting the trial transcript into a digital format; Dillon Jones, for scanning all of the newspaper articles; and Jody Boland for hours of research on the Danner family tree. A big thank-you to Richard Brown for his assistance researching jail blueprints, the gallows and maps of Central Park; and Norman Miller and Drew Carter for accompanying me to the crime scene on multiple occasions. I would also like to thank the Gallatin History Museum for its support as I obsessed over this case, as well as the descendants of those related to the case with whom I was able to talk and interview. This is their heritage, and I am honored to have been able to share their history.

We may never know the true story. Maybe the light will shine more in one direction for you than for others. In any case, there is a question, and that is reason enough to tell his story. So, on behalf of Seth Danner…

INTRODUCTION

Q. Now, if you will, continue and tell us in your own way, Mr. Smith, what events followed.

A. Well, then, the next morning we were supposed to meet there at 11 o'clock in the forenoon, but we were busy, and we met down there about—somewhere around one thirty. Mrs. Danner showed us where the bodies were. That was about quarter to two—1.45.

Q. Of what day?

A. The 18th day of June.

Q. 1923?

A. 1923. So then I dug around—prodded around, and I stirred up a leg. Then I notified the Coroner.

The sky was cloudy, a slight wind giving the sixty-degree weather a bit of a chill, especially where the road breaks out into the open fields of Montana. It was June 1923. From Bozeman, it's a thirty-mile drive to Three Forks, down a dirt road known as the famous "Yellowstone Trail," with the small towns of Belgrade, Central Park, Manhattan and Logan along the way.

It's about 1:30 in the afternoon when a police car pulls off the road halfway between Belgrade and Manhattan, just a few thousand feet from Central Park. Another car containing a man in uniform and a young woman is already parked there, having come from the opposite direction in Three Forks. In the full group are Three Forks deputy sheriff Pierce Elmore,

The crime scene grave site. Originally published in *True Detective* magazine, July 1935. *Gallatin Historical Society/Gallatin History Museum.*

Gallatin County sheriff Jim Smith, Deputy Max Howell and a Mrs. Iva Danner. The latter leads the men from the road through thick tangled underbrush less than ninety feet. They pick their way past disturbed ground, where the ghosts of two tents remain in the odd way grass comes back through trampled earth. Iva stops and points to a waterlogged depression in the ground, telling the men to "dig there." Equipped with a stick, Smith begins to prod the indicated earth beneath a few feet of water. It's uncertain whether he is skeptical of the woman's story or not, although Elmore was certainly moved enough to give him a call. Nothing had been found the two previous times Elmore had been out there, once just the night before, when he had asked Smith to meet him there. Suddenly, something comes to the surface, and there is no mistaking what it is: a human leg bone.

Smith feels more confident now of having brought Seth Danner, Iva's husband, to the Gallatin County Jail the night before. Then, it had been as a precaution; now, it seems it was a necessity. Smith moves the group away from the depression, sending Deputy Max Howell to Bozeman with Iva, where an official statement will be taken in the presence of an attorney and to notify the coroner in Bozeman. When Coroner E.W. Harland arrives, the digging is commenced, revealing the bodies of two unknown people lying side by side in a shallow grave. As the bodies make their way to Bozeman, they pass a deputy and Iva, who are headed back to her home in Three Forks after taking an official statement. Iva, seeing the conveyance, reportedly faints.

In less than twenty-four hours, her story is on the front page of the *Bozeman Avant Courier*: "Conscience-Stricken Wife Tells of Husband's Brutal Murders." The obscure Danners quickly become household names, dominating the press for the next year. Her story would appear in its near entirety four times prior to the trial, while Seth's would only appear in small fragments. The headlines read like a cross between a detective novel and a soap opera:

> *Slew Married Pair with Camper's Axe, Wife's Accusation*
> *Accused Slayer Says He Loves Wife Who Told*
> *Danner Used Murder Axe as Household Tool*
> *Slayer's Wife Tells Why She Revealed Crime*
> *Fear of Husband Not Conscience Led to Avowal*
> *Mrs. Danner Is Stepdaughter Accused Slayer*

Nowhere was the story told in full. Nowhere was Seth Danner given the benefit of the doubt. He was "guilty" with the very first headline.

PART I
LIFE AND CRIME

DANNER A HUMAN SPHYNX

Early Life of Seth Danner, May 1882–Fall 1919

Q. Your name is Seth Orrin Danner, is it?
A. Absolutely. The only one I ever had.

The dramatized storytelling of the newspapers would condemn Seth Danner far before the jury did, but this would be just the tip of the iceberg. Along with racial profiling (due to his supposed Cherokee blood), Seth would be accused of robbing Iva's innocence and committing incest and have his head literally examined in a phrenology test, which determined that his mental capacity was that of an underdeveloped prehistoric man. The press was endlessly fascinated by him, detailing his eating regimen, general health and religious conversations with guards and visitors. While some of the man's character is apparent, very little was actually known about his early life. A *Bozeman Weekly Chronicle* article detailing his death in 1924 ended with the subtitle "Danner's Inherent Cruelty." It was noted that, as a child, Seth had packed a door handle into a snowball and thrown it at another child, who, as a grown man, "never did get well from that snowball fight." According to the article: "As the man stood on the scaffold awaiting the final exit, the extreme paleness of his face brought out the cruel lines which revealed his character, as the people believe it to be. The story of his life is full of incidents wherein he had shown complete indifference to the pain of others. Human beings and animals are included in the list. He took pleasure in seeing others suffer."[1]

This was to be his portrayal in the press, and unfortunately there are few who can give light to any other part of the man or the truth of this analysis of his character. Most of his life boils down to the facts, the places he lived, the jobs he took on and the times he got into trouble. At the time of Seth's arrest, he was forty-one years of age, but as noted by many, he didn't look it. He had "every appearance of living most of his life in the open."[2]

Seth was born in Rooks County, Kansas, on May 15, 1882, to Amos and Eldora (Cool) Danner. He was the oldest of three children. Lucy Elizabeth was born in 1887, and Vernessa Mabel was born in 1889. His father was a farmer who spent almost his whole life in Kansas. It seems that Seth spent a good deal of time around his uncle, Ira Berton Danner, who also lived in Kansas.

On August 7, 1901, the *Philipsburg Herald*, based out of Philipsburg, Kansas, reported that two men, Vernon R. Stanfield and Bert Danner, Seth's uncle, had been killed in a well accident. It seems Bert had been in the well when he was overcome by noxious gases. His employer, Vernon, attempted to save Bert, but instead they both fell to the bottom of the well and were killed by either the fall, drowning or the gases. The article went on to report the death of Bert's wife as a result of shock, but this proved to be untrue. Within a year, Seth and his former aunt, Nancy Alice (Overholser) Danner, would marry, making Seth stepfather to his cousins, Ira (age five) and Iva (two). Iva had a twin who was either stillborn or died shortly after birth. At the time of their marriage, Seth was twenty-two and Nancy was twenty-five years old.

In 1907, their first son, Clyde F., was born, followed two years later by Benjamin Woodrow. Their daughter Florence was born in 1913. The couple lived a nomadic life, moving from place to place, doing odd jobs until 1915, when Nancy passed away from appendicitis at the young age of thirty-six, leaving Seth to "fight the battles of life alone" with five children.[3] Following the death of her mother, Nancy, Iva went to live with her uncle, possibly J.E. Overholser. At some point within the year, Iva contacted Seth, and the two left with Florence under cover of night, leaving the two boys behind. (See family tree, page 7).

By December 1916, they were located in Dillon, Montana, and in trouble. Danner was arrested on November 13, 1916. It seems the town didn't approve of Seth traveling with an unmarried pregnant woman. At this date, Iva was about eight months pregnant with her first child. The father seemed to be unknown, according to Seth. Years later, in an interview, Seth stated that Iva had contacted him for help to get her out of Kansas, because she was in trouble, and he obliged. In this scenario, the child was not his. In

Dillon, however, he was forced to marry Iva or spend a lot more time in jail. On December 23, 1916, the couple was married, the certificate claiming Iva was eighteen years and five months old. In truth, Iva was probably closer to the age of fifteen. Della Eldora was born the next day.

In Dillon, Seth worked as a machinist at the Dillon Auto Company during the rush seasons. According to the *Dillion Examiner*, Seth was an expert machinist but became quarrelsome and abusive when drunk, which it was said was often.[4] It seems Seth had been arrested in Dillon on an assault charge after he pulled a gun in a saloon, for which he served seventeen days in jail. The Danners would not remain in Dillion for long. In spring 1917, the Danners moved to Ruby, where Seth worked in another garage until the fall, when threshing season started and he got a quick job in Wilsall. By late 1917, they had moved on to Ennis, Iva working in a restaurant and Seth driving a truck. The following year became a haze of travel and quick work. Their time was spent at the McAfee Ranch, where Iva cooked for the men and Seth drove a tractor; Livingston, where Seth is listed in the city directory as a machinist at H.L Cummings and Son; and Yellowstone Park, where Seth spent at least two weeks, work unknown. It appears that they

Map of Montana, 1927, showing the locations where the Danners lived throughout their travels. *Gallatin Historical Society/Gallatin History Museum.*

also spent time in Bozeman for several months between 1917 and 1918, Seth working at Motor Sales on Black Avenue South. It was noted that he was a good "garage man and well liked." It was also mentioned that "he is said to have been so strong that he never troubled to use a jack to lift a Ford, but would raise it with one hand, then place the jack under for support while working on it."[5] By July 1919 they had headed back east to South Dakota, first spending a week in Cottonwood Lake, then Garland Park during the threshing season in the fall of 1919. Iva later stated that her second child, Marvin Eugene, was born in Garland Park that year.

Following the threshing season of 1919, the Danners moved to Britton, South Dakota. Seth found work at Roots Garage as a machinist and trapped on the side. The next spring, the family became acquainted with John and Florence Sprouse, a couple who lived nearby. Inspired by the Sprouses' wish to go west, and neither liking South Dakota much, Iva and Seth decided to head back to Montana that fall on what would be a fateful trip.

2

FROM MOBRIDGE, SOUTH DAKOTA, TO CENTRAL PARK, MONTANA

Traveling West with the Sprouses, Fall 1920

S.O. Danner, being first duly sworn, deposes and says that he was acquainted with John Sprouse and his wife Florence Sprouse; that he last saw them at Garland Park, South Dakota, in the fall of 1919 or 1920; that soon thereafter I, together with my wife, left for Montana by automobile, and arrived in Gallatin County in November, 1920.
—*Plaintiffs Exhibit No. 2, Statement made by Seth Danner, June 9, 1923*[6]

Seth first met John Sprouse at Roots Garage, where they both were employed. When later asked if John was a mechanic, Seth stated, "why, he was supposed to be…he wasn't much of an automobile mechanic. He was a good steam engineer."[7] John was a bit older than Seth, probably about forty to forty-two at the time of their meeting. The two men would borrow money from each other, each being in a similar financial situation, although Seth had children to care for and John did not. John's wife, Florence, may have been a mother in a previous marriage, but the child was not with them at the time. John was a divorced man with one child he had left behind. While Seth and John spent a good deal of time together, their wives, Iva and Florence, were relative strangers until the trip west.

John Sprouse had met his second wife, Florence, while working at a garage in Yam Hill, Oregon, where they had worked at the same garage, Florence as a bookkeeper. Her first husband's name had been O'Hara, but it was unclear how the marriage had ended. In one telling, Florence had an affair with John, and the two had run away together, fearing her husband's wrath. Both Seth and Iva would attest to Florence's fear of her former husband.

The Sprouses had left Britton a bit earlier, taking John's mother, Alpa Sprouse, to Fire Steel, South Dakota, and spending a few days with her. On the stand, Alpa mentioned that she knew that her son was going to be traveling with another family but did not recall the name, although she stated, "I am quite positive they spoke the name Danner; but I would not say…." That was the last anyone in South Dakota would hear of John and Florence Sprouse. While Florence had been known to write to her mother-in-law on occasion, the couple did not seem to have sent any correspondence on this particular journey. In fact, Florence had written her every week during their time in nearby Britton, but the letters had been destroyed years before, and little could be remembered about their contents or if the Danners had ever been mentioned.

Following the threshing season of 1920, Seth decided to again head to Montana. According to Iva, she did not know the Sprouses were also going to Montana, but it would appear that Seth and John had made some kind of plan to meet up, unbeknownst to her. The first stop that Iva could remember was Mobridge, South Dakota; remembered because it was there the Danners met up with the Sprouses. The next morning, the two cars set out, with the Sprouses in the lead. The two families would be on the road for the next two weeks, camping out along the way and at times preparing meals together. Both traveled in Fords; the Sprouses', however, was a touring car that had been cut down to make way for a truck bed for carrying supplies, which Iva stated was precious little. Along with the supplies, the Sprouses had a fox terrier.

The only places along the trip that could be remembered by Iva at the trial were a campsite along the Shield's River near Livingston, Montana; a night spent at Rocky Fork; and the final stop at Central Park. One could drive straight from Massachusetts to Washington on the Yellowstone Trail, the first transcontinental highway across the United States. The trail was first planned by J.W. Parmley of Ipswitch, South Dakota, in 1912, when automobile travel had begun to steadily rise. This portion of the trail near Central Park, however, is desolate, cutting through fields and wetlands running parallel to the Northern Pacific rail line. Between Bozeman and Three Forks were small, scattered towns supported by agriculturally driven families who had been in the valley for generations: Belgrade, Central Park, Manhattan and Logan. While the trail had brought a new stream of traffic into these small towns, the area was used to the tourist trade, belonging to the list of rare places where the land offers up both scenic beauty and good soil for crops. The water was good, too, supporting a number of breweries, including the Lerkinds. That is, supporting the industry until Prohibition swept the nation. The Roaring Twenties was not quite the era of "good times" for Montanans. In fact, the Great Depression hit Montana a decade before the rest of the nation, and one could say that the Danners and Sprouses were products of this situation. They went where the work took them and made just enough to get by.

The couples traveled together for most of the trip but on a few occasions became separated. It occurred once outside of Montana, but the Danners soon caught up with the Sprouses somewhere between Fallon and Billings. They found the Sprouses on that occasion broke down in the middle of the road with a busted crankshaft. According to Seth, he was eager to help and ended up purchasing the needed parts to get the Sprouse car back in order. By the time the trip was over, Seth stated that Sprouse owed him $113.

It was noted that Seth had chosen the camping spot on the afternoon they pulled into Central Park, but it is unclear why the travelers decided to stay longer than one night, as was their custom the previous few weeks. It was, however, determined the following day that the trapping was good, which

Three Forks area, fifteen miles from Central Park, showing the local landscape that was great trapping grounds for the Danners and Sprouses. *Gallatin Historical Society/Gallatin History Museum.*

may have been reason enough for the extended stay. From the latter part of October through the middle of November, Seth and John trapped from 9:00 a.m. to about 4:00 p.m., selling the hides in Bozeman.

In 1923, the *Bozeman Daily Chronicle* would list the men who had seen John and Seth, or, as one man called them, "Jack and Dan." The number of men was five and included W.C. Dyke, a trapper; Robert McClelland, a local farmer who was asked about renting a house by one of the men; Harry Collett and Harry Collett Jr., the latter of whom worked for the county at the time and was approached about a job by one of the men; and Ed Saville, who met the men on one occasion. Thus, the interactions John and Seth had with the community were scarce, not including those they met selling hides. The information on the women was even more scarce; they had mostly only been seen from a distance. Without a doubt, though, the Sprouses' and Danners' existence was known to some extent. Clearly, little notice was taken when, in November 1920, the Danners moved to Three Forks and the Sprouses simply disappeared.

THREE FORKS MEN HAD SOME MOON

Life in Gallatin County, January 1921–June 1923

*You must remember that you done things that was not right, and I did not
turn you down cold like you have me....I know just as well what you are
intending to do as you do. Now baby, it is not going to work, and don't forget
it....From the one you once loved.*
—*Seth Danner, May 24, 1923*

Life in Three Forks was quiet for the first two years the Danners lived
there. They had turned up in the little town late in the afternoon of
November 17. Seth had quickly found work in the garage of Ed Avery as
a truck driver, but as times were hard, life was hard. In later testimonies, it
would be discovered that community members had given food and clothing
to the Danner children and Iva, who were living in near destitution.

Seth first drew the attention of the area when, on April 21, a Constable
Kaiser and Deputy Sheriff Pierce Elmore of Three Forks picked up S.L.
Seagraves and Seth on a possession of moonshine charge. Seagraves
pleaded guilty and was fined $150 by Judge Ben Law. Seth, however, was in
big trouble; items had been discovered at the Danner home that matched
a recent theft.

The story eventually became more confused when the details of the
Seagraves trial were shared in the *Bozeman Daily Chronicle*. According to
the paper, Seth had been brought on as a state's witness, testifying that
Seagraves had come to his home on the evening of the thefts (March
23, 1923) and asked Seth to take a ride with him. They both drank a

Avery Garage in Three Forks, photo taken in 1925 following a major earthquake. *Gallatin Historical Society/Gallatin History Museum.*

"quantity of moonshine whiskey and consumed all they had with them while making the trip toward to the Steven's ranch." As it turned out, Seagraves had recently gotten into an argument with Stevens over some wages not paid. Upon arrival at the ranch, Seagraves went into the barn, removing several pieces of tack, including harnesses and saddles, stating, "I guess that will make up for what they owe me." Seagraves had put the stuff in his own cellar; however, the articles were found just days later outside the Danner home in a manure pile. At the trial, Iva also was called as a witness; surprisingly, she stood by Seth, claiming to have no knowledge of the items found. She even testified to Seagraves telling her that the officers had "found the right goods, but not the right place," which was denied by Seagraves. The Danners' story was discounted, and Seagraves was released, having served his time for the bootlegging crime.[8]

Seth had already pleaded guilty on the bootlegging and larceny charge a few months before the Seagraves trial. The search of the Danner home for the stolen goods had illuminated another crime; Seth's family was found to be in extreme need of food and clothing, and Seth was now looking at a charge of nonsupport. When it came down to it, Seth was sentenced to "not less than 5 years nor more than ten years" in the state prison at Deer Lodge but was paroled by Judge Law so he could provide for his family. The provisions were that Seth get a steady job in Bozeman and that he support his wife and children.[9]

Confiscated still items sitting outside the county jail during Prohibition in the 1920s. *Gallatin Historical Society/Gallatin History Museum.*

The job, found by Judge Law, was at L.K. Pence's garage. According to the *Bozeman Daily Chronicle*, Judge Law told the man "to keep working and in time he could get himself a little home in Bozeman and move his family up here."[10] It seems the judge saw some potential in the character of Seth Danner. For several weeks, Seth worked at the garage, often sending letters to his wife in Three Forks and on occasion paying visits on his motorcycle. Things seemed to be looking up, until June 7, when Iva Danner came to Deputy Sheriff Elmore as a "conscience-stricken"[11] woman with a sordid tale.

A few days following the reveal of the murders, one of the letters written by Seth to his wife was published in the *Daily Chronicle* and seemed to suggest that maybe everything wasn't as peaceful as it may have seemed from the outside. The middle part of the letter suggests some secret between the two and, interestingly, foreshadows a hangman's noose:

> *Now don't let Elmore talk you into nothing more. How can you leave me and listen to other people, and mind them and disobey me, dear little sweetheart. How can you treat me that way. I wouldn't do you that way if*

I was hanged. You must remember that you done things that was not right, and I did not turn you down cold like you have me. As to what they said about me staying all night with you, the judge said it was all right, that my parole was up and it was nobody's business but mine, and they are just feeding you taffy to get you to quit me. If you listen to other people you will never live with me again. I know just as well what you are intending to do as you do. Now baby, it is not going to work, and don't forget it.[12]

The letter ended with the instructions to "burn this letter." It would appear that Seth had some inkling of what his wife may have planned— in short, to turn him in for the murders and rid herself of him in the process. In light of the two stories that would emerge later on as to what had happened out there, this letter could be read in multiple ways and does not necessarily prove any guilt. Probably the most prophetic line, however, was in the first paragraph, where Seth pleads, "Don't, don't, for God's sake, tell everything you know."

The bulk of the rest of the letter was about his daughter Florence, who was at that time an invalid. The tone is religious, with lines like, "Put your trust in the Lord and He will do the rest" and "Tell little Florence that daddy still loves her, and she must pray too." He also instructs Iva that if she would spend more time in prayer and worship there would be less time to hatch plans to "send me over the road." There is also some question of a gun, but it is unclear why Iva had been asking about one.

The end of the letter contradictorily shows Seth's warning of betrayal and resignation to Iva's plans.

Well, girlie, it is after 10 o'clock and I will have to close and go to bed by myself and cry my cry out. How you can treat me this way and think you are doing right, is more than I can tell. I could not think of doing you that way. But if God tells you it is right, go right ahead and do it until you are tired. Here is hoping that he will show you where you are wrong. Well, baby, good night, and may God bless and keep you and my little ones, is my prayer. From the one you once loved. S. O. D. xxxxxxx. Tell little Florence that daddy still loves her and she must pray too. May God bless her.[13]

This was only one of many letters written but was the only one published in the paper, clearly because of the allusion to something sinister. The newspaper stated that this letter in particular is to be "looked upon as important, for it leads to the conclusion that Danner is fearful of leaving his

Employees of the Pence garage photographed just one year following Seth's employment, 1924. *Gallatin Historical Society/Gallatin History Museum.*

wife alone lest she tell things which were secrets of themselves alone." The letter did little to silence the determined woman, however. Within a month, her story was out of the bag.[14]

One day following the discovery of the bodies, the press reported the whole story, Iva's story, in an article titled "Conscience-Stricken Wife Tells of Husband's Brutal Murders." The article detailed the history of the Sprouses and the Danners in the "remarkable story of a double crime."[15] In 2,304 words, the woman's saga was recounted and Seth was very nearly condemned.

Iva's story would be the same reiterated at the trial; she would never waver in her telling of the events that had occurred. According to Iva, late on the evening of November 14, Seth had come back alone from checking the trap lines with John. When Florence Sprouse asked about her husband, Seth told her they had split up by the river and he hadn't seen him since. Iva was preparing fish for dinner, and Seth went about gathering wood for the night, asking Florence if she needed any. Florence said she was fine on wood till her husband came home and answered the same when Seth asked again later on.[16]

As time passed and night began to fall, Florence became more agitated over her missing husband, even running toward a passing car and the sound of someone hollering, thinking it might be John lost in the woods. Seth had followed her to the fence, then they both turned back around, Iva turning around early so that her back was to the two. As she went into her tent, she caught a view in her peripheral vision of Seth reaching down for the hand ax then heard the sound of a blow, but she hadn't looked back to see what it had been as she continued into the tent. Almost immediately, Seth called her back out. Iva claims to have come out to see Seth on top of the woman with his hand around her neck and the ax in his other hand. He asked Iva to give him a "whang string" (a length of leather string), which he then tied tightly around Florence's neck. The blow had apparently not been sufficient to kill her, but she was most likely in a very serious condition.[17]

Fifteen to twenty minutes passed before Seth exclaimed, "Now, I reckon she'll know where Jack is now" before he picked up the woman and placed her in her own tent. Seth then went to his own tent and ate his supper. They went to bed, Iva not sleeping on account of the trauma of the act that had just ensued. She heard Seth get up and dig for a bit then go out early from the camp. When he came back, he got Iva up to make him breakfast before he went over his trap lines like normal. Upon his return, he asked Iva if she wanted to see John, and he led her to the Sprouse tent, where both bodies now lay. According to Iva, John had a gunnysack tied about his head. His boots had been off, and his clothes had icicles on them. Seth threatened her never to tell, lest she end up like the Sprouses. Supposedly, at some point, he told her that he had killed John for money with a shotgun, but she seemed to know nothing more.[18]

Seth spent the day going through the Sprouses' belongings, keeping a few things while throwing most items in a giant fire. The children were kept inside of their tent, easily done since they hadn't shoes and the weather was cold. They were told that the Sprouses had hopped a night train back to South Dakota. That night, Seth buried the Sprouses, Iva stating that she saw the bodies of John and Florence Sprouse in the grave. The next day, they traveled into Three Forks, where they had remained all these years.[19] Seth and Seagraves had been held at the county jail together that June. Seth had since been picked up for murder, and Seagraves had been finishing out his bootlegging sentence. At some point, Seagraves inquired of Seth, "Why didn't you fill that motorcycle full of gas and just keep going?" Seth replied, "I didn't think they'd find them."[20]

When the article mentioned that Seth was "safely locked in the county jail," it feels as though the area was meant to breathe a sigh of relief that this murderer was locked up and not roaming loose throughout the town. The last line of the article goes to show the general attitude toward Seth, demonizing him by his possible race: "Danner is said to have Indian blood in his veins. He originally came from Oklahoma, and admits being part Cherokee."[21]

Of note, a few times it was surmised that Florence had been pregnant at the time of her death. This announcement in the papers would make the murder of the woman even more atrocious. However, at the trial, no mention was made of an unborn child, which surely an autopsy would have revealed. Thus, the reference to her pregnancy must have been falsely printed.

The story nevertheless was brutal. If it was true, Iva had grounds for trying to get clear of this murderous man through a divorce. The alleged crime could not be grounds for divorce, so the attempt would be made to plead for brutality and neglect. But one couldn't help but pity a woman who had lived in apparent fear for three years. Everyone was interested in hearing what this woman had to say, even at the divorce trial, for all knew the outcome would greatly affect the murder trial to come. Even Iva herself was interested in the newspaper coverage, making clippings of all references to the Danner case.[22]

An article published the next day tried to show Seth's side of the case but seems more like an opportunity to publish the words of a murderer than a pursuit of the truth. It was noted that Seth had been getting ready for his Saturday bath (the kind of details that readers ate up) when he met with the newspapermen. According to the article, Seth "smiled and asked what was wanted, and then admitted that he supposed he knew, since he had read his wife's story as published in all the papers."[23] The first portion of the article contained 762 words in which Seth denied knowing anything about the double murders. He emphatically spoke of a mystery man, Florence Sprouse's first husband, who was out to get his unfaithful wife and take Iva in the process. The next 1,510 words again detailed Iva's story and the discovery of the bodies at Central Park.

On June 11, 1923, Seth pleaded "not guilty" to the murder charges at the Gallatin County Courthouse with a cigarette in his mouth, a "breach of etiquette" that was ignored.[24] It was little notes like the cigarette that seemed to interest readers. The public was anxious to know all about the man behind bars, but they appeared to be much more interested in his appearance and odd statements than in his side of the story. It was noted that while he was carefree during the daytime, when jailers and visitors alike could see him;

at night, he would pace up and down his cell. Apparently, when caught, he would state that he had just gotten up.[25]

Since practically everyone in the valley knew of the crime and all had a basic knowledge of where it had been committed, it was quite humorous when a report came in that just one day after the bodies had been discovered, a group of tourists had been picnicking at the camping ground near Central Park. The unassuming group had made their unsavory discovery when reporters from the *Chronicle* arrived to take photos of the crime scene. According to the paper, a lady member of the party exclaimed, "Scene of the WHAT?" to which the reporter tactfully informed the tourists that "they had just enjoyed their luncheon on the site of the most brutal murders in Montana's history." The tourists, from South Dakota and Arkansas, quickly made their exit.[26]

This bout of humor was followed with an editorial-like article begging the questions: "What moved Iva Danner to confess husband's crimes?" "Was it conscience?" "If not conscience, what prompted her at this late date to make her gruesome confession?" and "Was it robbery, as Mrs. Danner says?" The idea of a woman's conscience seemed inadequate to the author, who states: "It was a horrible secret to carry for two years and a half. Iva Danner saw her husband kill Flossie Sprouse with a hatchet—and she didn't tell. She saw the body of big John Sprouse, a gunny sack over the shot-riddled head. And she didn't tell. If conscience prompted Iva Danner to tell her story, thus sending her husband to prison and almost certainly sending him to death if her story proves true, then her brain has been a battleground for two and a half years." This is a valid point. What could have prompted such a sudden and definite turn in her mind?[27]

The article targeted the motive as the most important aspect of the case, something that would be seemingly lost in the murder trial to come. To the author of the article, the motive of robbery seemed unlikely, noting that John Sprouse did not appear wealthy, as he was living the itinerate farmer lifestyle and owned only a Ford car, just like the one owned by Danner. The author questioned the likelihood of a man committing two brutal murders for a second Ford car and the little money that may have been hidden in one's boots. Only an insane man could commit such an act, and it was noted that Seth was not deemed insane by anyone who had known him. Amid all the questions of motive and conscience, the author asked perhaps the most pertinent question: "When these questions are answered, the threads of the most gruesome pit murder story in Montana's history will have been woven into a noose—for whom?"[28]

This would be the defining question of the case: Which person—husband or wife—was telling the truth?

PART II

COURTROOM DRAMA

DANNER FIGHTS DIVORCE ACTION OF CHILD WIFE

The Danner Divorce Trial, August 1923

Mrs. Danner has great fear of Danner, yet she is anxious to be near him. Her quarters are within a few feet of his cell, which is on the floor below....She says it makes her feel badly to hear him sing, but she listens, nevertheless, and does not go away when he bursts into song or plays. She said she used to play the piano and he would play the banjo with her.
—Bozeman Daily Chronicle, *June 16, 1923*

J ust one day after the appearance of Iva's confession in the papers and two days after the discovery of the bodies, Danner was interviewed by the *Bozeman Daily Chronicle.* He was asked why his wife had told her story, and Danner quickly produced a copy of the complaint in which Iva had started proceedings for a divorce. He stated, "That's the reason and the reason why she wants to get rid of me is because of another man somewhere."[29] However, the "mystery man" would remain a mystery for quite some time yet. He would turn out to be James Troglia and come to be known as "Jim the Baker" in the murder trial proceedings. In this first mention of divorce, it was noted that Iva's grounds were on "failure to support" and that she wanted custody of the children. In time, she would care little for the children, seeming all too ready to let the state take care of them.

Things quickly became more entangled for Iva when, a week later, a story broke about a "joy party" of which Iva had been a participant. Coincidently, the day that Iva revealed her long-held secret to the police had been the same day that a Mr. Jack Brown had filed for a divorce. The basis of his

Downtown Three Forks. *Gallatin Historical Society/Gallatin History Museum.*

suit was infidelity. It seems he had been informed of a party being thrown at the home of another man in Three Forks, and when he went to break it up with a gun in hand, he found the room dark, his wife hidden under the bed and a woman at the door. A man had slipped through a window. It was later disclosed that the woman at the door had indeed been Iva Danner. The *Daily Chronicle* notes that Iva, "realizing there would be much gossip over the escapade, and that tales of the affair might reach her husband, who was still working in Bozeman," decided "she had better carry out her intentions of 'breaking loose' from him at once."[30] The man whose home it was turned out to be James Troglia. It was also noted that Iva may have had a discussion with Mrs. Brown following the party, during which Mrs. Brown mentioned something about murder. It may have been enough for Iva to return to the Brown home soon after and tell enough of her story to bolster confidence in telling all to the police. Either way, it seems the breaking up of the party had been somewhat influential to Iva in sharing her story.

The next mention of divorce was from Danner himself, in a paragraph on his life thus far at the jail. The paper stated that his only care seemed to be that "mamma should try and get a divorce from me."[31] It wouldn't be until June 30 that the divorce case would start to see regular reporting. A demurrer was filed by Danner's lawyer just a day before the twenty-day limit for objections was up. The objection was to Iva's claim of cruelty. It still seemed that the impending divorce was the most important thing on Seth's mind. He was quoted by the paper: "I never did anything to mama that she should want to get a divorce from me. I don't care about the other charges against me [meaning the murder charges]. What makes me feel bad is that she should want to get rid of me. If she gets her divorce, I have nothing more to live for. I love her better than I do my life, and there isn't anything I wouldn't do for her. Even now, I would take her back and forgive everything she has done."[32]

The paper acknowledged how important the outcome of the divorce case would be in determining how the murder trial proceeded. Iva could not testify against her husband if still married to him, and her testimony was very nearly the only thing that condemned Seth for the murders. Without her, the case might be lost. Surprisingly, Judge Law sustained the demurrer, making Seth and the defense victors in the first round. County Attorney E.A. Peterson was asked to submit an amended bill with specific details as to the charge of cruelty. They were quickly supplied. According to the amendment, dates and witnesses were listed that proved Danner's abuse and mistreatment of Iva and the family. In particular, one instance was mentioned in which Seth had come home with a gun, threatening to kill Iva. According to the paper, she had "begged for mercy and while running about the room of her home trying to dodge bullets, finally quieted her husband."[33] She had been able to show officials where the bullet holes were in the room and at the piano where a key had been chipped. Again, it was ascertained that without Iva's testimony, the murder case would be built on circumstantial evidence only. It was noted at this time that Frank Sprouse, brother of the deceased John Sprouse, was on his way to help investigators with the case.

Meanwhile, the children were sent to the state home in Twin Bridges. Previously, they had been living in town with a Mrs. Neely, county matron. On occasion, they had been allowed to come to the jail to visit and play with their father: "They were taken into the inside corridor and he was allowed to come out, where for a quarter of an hour he played with them and otherwise petted them."[34] At this time, Della was six, Marvin three and Donald one and a half years old. Seth's daughter Florence, who was ten years old, was in such poor health that she was under care at the Deaconess Hospital, where she had an unfortunate accident in a laundry mechanism. A place had to be found for the children, as Iva had been brought into the custody of the sheriff's department just days after Seth's arrest. She was held as a witness and could come and go as she pleased but had to spend nights at the jail.[35]

Photo of Marvin Danner with the caption: "Grandpa Danner with his new wagon!" *Photo courtesy Janet (Danner) Mann, granddaughter.*

Weeks later, it was stated that the Danner children were going to live with their uncle J.E. Overholser in Spokane. He was the brother of Seth's first wife, Alice. On Florence's leaving she was allowed to visit her father, Seth, in the jail. Florence asked Seth when he would be visiting her in Washington, to which he replied: "I may never see you again. Our family is all broken up now, and after what mama has done, I don't care anymore. But you keep on loving your mama, and never forget to love your daddy."[36] This article in the *Bozeman Daily Chronicle* ended with the statement that Mr. Overholser felt "keenly the disgrace of Danner."[37] However, it seems that only Florence went to live with the Overholsers.

The next mention of the divorce case came on August 17, now over a month since the Danner family had come to be known locally by all. Most of the article surrounded Seth's insistence that he had been a "dutiful husband" who had provided for his family to the utmost of his ability. While the article does give Seth a voice, it was titled "Danner Fights Divorce Action of Child Wife." If one only read the headline, the image of Danner as a husband and father would be lost in the innuendo. The article went on to state that Danner did not consider his wife fit to care for the children; he wished to provide the care they needed himself. It is clear in all of his interactions with

DANNER FIGHTS DIVORCE ACTION OF CHILD WIFE

Denies He Had Ever Been Cruel to Her or Children. Always Willing and Ready to Support Family.

Newspaper headline, *Bozeman Daily Chronicle*, August 17, 1923. *Gallatin Historical Society/Gallatin History Museum.*

his children that he either cared for them deeply or was a wonderful actor able to trick those who were watching; namely, the press. By most accounts, the former seems more likely, although his judgment on life choices definitely left the children affected on more than one occasion. Cruelty to the children was never mentioned. His only transgression toward them appears to be his inability to provide them with the essentials for life. But one must also remember the era in which they lived; life was hard for many.[38]

Iva had taken a liking to her newfound independence. Without children to worry about and without a man to provide for her, she managed to get a job at a restaurant. It was said that she bought herself "some good clothes," which she claimed to have never had before.[39]

The divorce trial was finally held on August 25, attracting a large audience, as the outcome of this trial could determine the outcome of the murder trial to follow. In fact, the courtroom was filled long before the trial was to start, most expecting to hear both Iva and Seth speak on the stand. But only Iva spoke that day, called as the first witness. In her testimony, she recounted the details of their marriage, the birth of the children and their lifestyle in general.

County Attorney Peterson questioned Iva as to how Seth had supported her in their married life, to which she answered:

> *There was no time during our married life that he supported me or the children as he should. We always just existed and never had enough to eat. While we lived at Three Forks, the children never had sufficient clothing, and many times we had to subsist on bread and water. During the winters we were often destitute for clothing, and the children would have to go barefoot. I haven't had a new dress in two years, and about all of the clothing I ever did have was given some by other women who took pity on me.* "[40]

In later testimony, all of these points would be acknowledged by others in the community, including a Mrs. William Veach, who stated that she had brought food and clothing to the family, finding the house in disrepair, with holes through the windows in the dead of winter. Veach stated that "Florence had frozen her feet and hands while going and coming from school, and her finger nails turned black and came off."[41] The Danners' destitution was confirmed by Deputy Sheriff Elmore of Three Forks, who had reported the situation to the county commissioners; Emma Koffus, who had sent food and clothing; and James Troglia; who had delivered the supplies from Koffus. As to the accusation of cruelty, Iva recounted the aforementioned stories of Seth shooting at her and the conditions in which her last two children had been born, the youngest of whom hadn't been under any medical attendance. There was also a mention of an incident with a new dress that Iva had acquired from a local woman over which Seth had allegedly choked and beat her. Seth's current record, which included conviction for a felony, was cited as evidence of his inability to support.[42]

In cross-examination by Attorney Smith, it was discovered that Iva had gotten into trouble in Britton, South Dakota, where she had taken some "old rags and quilts and some things from a woman" for which she had been arrested. Seth had gotten her out of jail. Smith also questioned Iva about the "other man" to which she denied any knowledge of. Ironically, the "other man" was sitting in the courtroom as a witness: James Troglia.[43]

No decision was made at the time the trial ended, as the court took the matter "under advisement" and would give its decision at a later time. It was noted that Seth was showing the effects of his long confinement, now having lasted more than two months. The *Chronicle* stated that Seth "looked sallow and soft. His swarthy complexion has gone, and he is getting flabby."[44] But it was also mentioned that he had remained cool and seemingly unaffected throughout the trial.

The result of the trial wouldn't be announced until Tuesday (the trial had been on Saturday), at which point Judge Law granted Iva a divorce from her husband. The three children were to stay under the care of the state, while Florence Danner was living with Mr. Overholser in Spokane, Washington, at the time. The *Bozeman Daily Chronicle* noted that, according to Iva, who had received a letter from her stepdaughter, Florence was to appear at the murder trial and help establish the fact that the Danners and Sprouses were indeed together at Central Park. This would counter Seth's earlier statement that he hadn't seen the Sprouses since South Dakota.[45]

Now that the divorce was final, all attention was put on the murder trial. After all, that had been the real interest in the Danners from the start.

CHAIN OF FACT DRAWS
TIGHTER AROUND DANNER

The Murder Trial, Day 1, October 22, 1923

I'd say hang him.
—*Prospective juror,* Bozeman Daily Chronicle, *October 1923*

Just days before the trial was to begin, Seth "piloted" his attorney, Justin Smith, over the Central Park site. It was the first time he had been off the city block that contained both the jail and the courthouse side by side. Seth was handcuffed to his attorney throughout the journey. The *Daily Chronicle* noted that "before leaving, the sheriff strapped his automatic around his waist."[46] When the group arrived, Seth pointed out the place where the tents had been and took them on a brief tour of the creek where, years before, he had trapped with John Sprouse. Seth and his attorney often talked between themselves, but nothing was captured of their conversation. It was noted that both left the area seemingly content with the journey. Upon their return, Attorney Smith commented that Seth would probably "go back, into his cell now and play the banjo and sing."[47]

At some point at Central Park, Seth remarked to the sheriff, "Jim, the first thing you know, you'll be minus a wheel on that gig of yours, the way you travel over these roads," in reference to the sixty-five miles per hour they had traveled for part of the journey.[48] At another time, he named the men in cars passing and told the sheriff where they were from and if they were bootleggers. He knew his way around a car and knew all the local "color." As with most mentions of Seth, the loss of his "rugged outdoor appearance and swarthiness" was taken into account.

The last time that Seth had been near the location was on the night of his arrest, June 7, for the alleged murders months earlier. On that occasion, Seth had driven a motorcycle while Deputy Howell had ridden in the sidecar. They had left Three Forks, where Seth had been picked up at his home, around 10:00 p.m., and arrived at the jail around midnight. The bodies of the Sprouses would not be found until the next morning, but Howell was certain Seth had known what he was being brought in for. According to Howell, Seth had inquired of him if he had his gun on him. When Howell said yes, Seth was noted as smiling as he stated, "There is a bad dog down the road a ways, and I wish you would get him." During the ride through the Central Park area, Seth's motorcycle had stopped several times, each time alarming Howell enough to keep his hand on his gun, alert to Seth's actions. Nothing occurred to substantiate Howell's fears, however, and Seth was soon in the custody of the jail.[49]

It seems there was now also a fear of Iva Danner. It was mentioned how the sheriff's department had locked Iva up in the women's quarters of the jail. Prior to the latter part of August, she had been in their custody but allowed to come and go as she pleased. Something had changed with the urgency of her testimony; it is possible the department thought Iva might run now that she had obtained her divorce. As it would turn out, County Attorney Peterson had requested that either the county pay Iva $1,000 following her testimony or they lock her up until the trial was over. This makes it very apparent that Peterson was aware of the danger of Iva's skipping town prior to the trial. Judge Law granted the petition, stating that it appeared to the court that "such a witness will not appear and testify unless security be required."[50] It would appear that the monetary deal had not been made and Iva had been placed under lock and key. But the legend of Iva's being paid to testify has remained in the Danner family line to the present day.

On October 22, the trial began. Seventy jurors were called forward for the Danner trial. They would be weeded through until twelve were chosen and sworn in. Those in the jury box were questioned by both County Attorney Peterson and Attorney General Rankin. According to the *Bozeman Daily Chronicle*, "in the examination of the jurors, every man was asked if he had conscientious scruples in fixing the death penalty, in case Danner was found guilty of the crime." Each juror was also asked if he would give more credence to Iva's testimony than Seth's if both were to take the stand, and if they were completely impartial to the case and to Seth. In fact, the question was formed for each juror "if his frame of mind, should he be accepted as a juror, was such that he could impartially try the case, and that, if his position

Gallatin County Courthouse. *Gallatin Historical Society/Gallatin History Museum.*

and that of Danner were reversed, he would accept Danner as a juror."[51] Several men were dismissed as they either opposed the death penalty or had formed opinions about the case due to its presence in the local papers. In all, thirty-four of the seventy were called, with seven dismissed for their stance on the death penalty.

It is important to note just how informed each juror already was on the case because of the proceeding months of coverage by the papers. As noted by the *Daily Chronicle* itself:

> *Interest in the Danner case has aroused not only the local community but that of the state and the adjoining states. In every hamlet, town and city, the people are eager for news regarding the crime which has so many startling and atrocious features connected with it. At first there seemed few who were not willing to judge Danner, but as the time for the trial approached, opinions have changed to some extent. This was evidenced in the examination of the jurors yesterday. Several of the men said they had formed opinions and had discussed them with others regarding the guilt of Danner. Further, they said they were willing to try the case upon its merits and would, if taken as jurors, have to be thoroughly convinced before adjudging him guilty.*[52]

There was not a juror who was not, to some depth, informed of the case. No one could have missed the coverage and general interest in the murders. While many said they could judge fairly given the evidence to come, their acknowledgement that they had formed opinions at one time or another on the case is rather alarming. One has only to look back at the headlines mentioned in the previous chapters to imagine what each juror had been exposed to in the course of the last few months. This is important to keep in mind. Could Seth have ever had a truly unbiased trial? This question was asked in the days following the verdict.

These proceedings took the whole of the morning and afternoon. Seth was present, but Iva was not. At one point during the interrogation of a juror, the man exclaimed that "if they bring evidence of guilty against this man, I'd say hang him," to which Danner smiled "broadly" and there was a "tittering in the courtroom," calling the judge to "rap for order."[53] It was noted that Seth "never flinched once during the first day's proceedings in court, and when the attorneys kept continually referring to 'the death penalty,' 'the heinous crime' and other subjects expected to trouble his conscience, he sat unmoved."[54]

At the close of the day, twenty prospective jurors were left, the final to be decided on the following day, which would be followed by Attorney Peterson's opening statements. The courtroom had been filled early with spectators, many of whom had drifted out during the morning, and it was again filled to capacity in the afternoon, with many again drifting out by the close of the day. All were awaiting the beginning of the trial itself and, in particular, the testimony of Iva Danner. It was also mentioned that the witnesses had arrived in town, including Florence Danner from Spokane, Frank Sprouse (brother of deceased John Sprouse) from Washington and Marvin and Mrs. Alpa Sprouse (brother and mother of deceased) from Mobridge, South Dakota.

Frank Sprouse had already been a large part of the murder investigation conducted by the sheriff's department. Frank had arrived in July, apparently of his own accord, to aid in the identification of his brother's personal effects. Many were found in the Danner home. According to Frank, the crime had been premeditated; it looked to him like "Danner had planned doing away with my brother and his wife for a long time. He shunned the regular tourist camps, the letter written home to mother was never found, and no trace whatever has been found of the two families having been together, while we know that they met at Mobridge and have absolute knowledge that they were together during the entire trip till the time of the disappearance."[55] Frank had then continued west to Yam Hill, Washington, where he continued his investigation. Florence had been from the area, and there was some question still of her former jealous husband. Nothing much must have been gained in that trip, however, as it was not mentioned again in any detail. Frank returned to Bozeman just days before the trial was to begin. In fact, his return was mandatory as an important witness to the state.

County Attorney Peterson had also made a journey, to South Dakota, where he met with the Sprouse family in the weeks before the trial. The information gained was not earth-shattering, and much had already been known. The one important item of note was the positive identification of the Sprouse car, which had been ascertained by the original owner of the car. There was no doubt that Seth had sold the Sprouse car in Montana. Of interest to many was the state of the Sprouse family, who were apparently "well-to-do" people, highly respected in their community. The same was said of the murdered man, John Sprouse.[56]

INTENSE INTEREST SHOWN

The Murder Trial, Day 2, October 23, 1923

MR. PETERSON: Now, Mr. Danner, do you understand that the questions which I am about to ask you and the answers which you will make thereto, concerning a certain investigation which the Sheriff's office has conducted near Central Park, may be used against you?

MR. DANNER: Yes, sir.

MR. PETERSON: Do you understand that the statement which you are about to make is made without the County Attorney's or the Sheriff's offering you any immunity or any promise whatsoever, that you are making this statement of your own free will?

MR. DANNER: Yes.

The trial itself finally started on October 23. That morning, the twelve jurors were settled on by eleven o'clock, leaving enough time for the opening statements to be made before the noon recess. Attorney Wellington D. Rankin was permitted to take charge of the prosecution with assistance by County Attorney Peterson. However, a surprise was unveiled when Rankin requested the entering of additional witnesses for the state without prior notification to Danner attorney Justin Smith. Smith objected, but Judge Law permitted the additions. The new witnesses were on hold to possibly testify to the fact that Seth had admitted to burying the bodies of the Sprouses following their deaths. This would prove that Seth had seen the Sprouses since Mobridge, South Dakota, in opposition to his long-held statement that he hadn't seen them since.

The first few witnesses for the state were brought on the stand that afternoon to describe the discovery of the bodies, establishing that a crime had been committed. Deputy Sheriff Pierce Elmore was called first, understandably, as his involvement was the first to signal there was something amiss near Central Park. After all, it was Elmore with whom Iva had felt comfortable enough to tell her sordid story, quite possibly the first to ever hear it in its entirety. Elmore told how his initial search of the area was unsuccessful and how Sheriff Smith had been called in to help. As Elmore had not been present when the full excavation of the bodies was completed, Smith was called to the stand to continue the story.

Smith noted that at 1:45 p.m., Iva had pointed out a place where the bodies should have been located. Within minutes of starting to dig about with a stick, Smith "stirred up a leg." This began a long and detailed conversation about the location of the bodies, amount of time between discovery and excavation and descriptions of the camping grounds.

The two bodies were lying south to north, with their heads south nearer the railroad tracks and their feet north toward the Yellowstone Trail. Little digging had been done to bury the bodies, as they had been placed in a natural depression in the ground and covered with stones and earth. In November, little water would have been there, but by the time they were removed three years later, in June, they were under nearly a foot and a half of water covered by brush.

Unfortunately, the exhibit drawings referred to throughout this early portion of the trial were destroyed during scheduled records disposal in the 1980s. This makes it difficult today to ascertain exactly where the locations were that they were discussing. In general, the location was averaged to be about 1,000 feet west of the Central Park bridge and centered about 200 feet north and south between the Yellowstone Trail road and the Northern Pacific rail line. The county surveyor, S.D. Waldorf, visited the area to confirm the presence of the bodies in Gallatin County and was the next witness called. According to Waldorf, the excavation where the bodies had been removed was 113 feet from the center of the railway track and 38 feet from the Northern Pacific right-of-way fence. Another 38 feet southwest was a small creek (see figure on page 48). Nearby were the remaining markings of a tent camp, within 10 feet of where the bodies had been buried. Deputy Sheriff E.M. Howell was called to support the testimony of both Elmore and Smith and was followed by the coroner.

Ellery Willis Harland was thirty-six years old and had been in the area since at least 1918. His business practice, first named Harland & Caven,

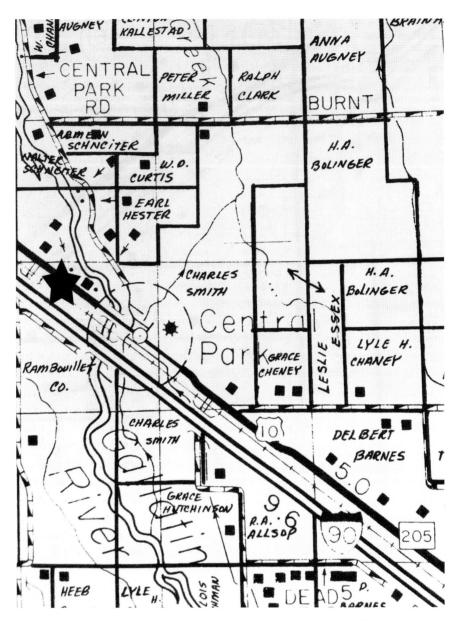

Map showing the vicinity of the Danners' campsite and the crime scene. The star toward the left side of the map labels the location. *Gallatin Historical Society/Gallatin History Museum.*

then just Harland by 1922, would have a short lifespan. In January 1925, Harland sailed for Australia for "business." By 1930, he was no longer in the area, nor was he an undertaker. The 1930 census finds him in Salem, Oregon, in the real estate business, where he would remain until his death in 1971. In 1924, Harland was the coroner of Gallatin County.

Once the leg bone was discovered, the area remained untouched until Harland arrived, roughly an hour following the initial discovery. Using pitchforks, the men were able to work the bodies out, removing first a gunnysack that pulled loose from the body of the man. Inside were a few pieces of the man's skull, which were removed from the sack. Once the man was pulled up, the woman was removed without much difficulty. Both were immediately placed in a basket and carried by Harland from there to Bozeman, where they were kept in the basement of his undertaking parlor until physicians could make their examination. Interestingly, the skulls of both were kept for the trial, but according to records, the bodies of Mr. and Mrs. Sprouse were buried in the Sunset Hills in county plots on June 15, 1923, nearly four months prior to the trial. One cannot help but wonder if the skulls were ever reunited in the burial plot.

It was determined through the coroner's testimony that Florence Sprouse had been a short, heavy woman, while her husband, John, had been tall, probably over six feet. Seth Danner would later describe John as being six feet, one inch, about 165 pounds, clean-shaven with a dark complexion and light eyes. He described Florence as less than five feet tall, a little heavy, with dark hair, although he wasn't certain about the hair color. Seth would also note that the Sprouses were roughly in their forties. Only one photo of the Sprouses emerged in the newspapers, the only one that survives to the present day. It is a bust portrait, making it difficult to tell the Sprouses' actual physiques. Harland's testimony was cut short, however, and resumed later in the trial. It seems that it had been assumed that Harland would bring the skulls with him, something he had been unaware of. Harland was excused to retrieve the skulls while a new witness was called.

Next on the stand was Peterson, the county attorney for Gallatin County. Peterson, Smith, Elmore, Howell and Harland had all started their office positions on January 1, 1923. Peterson testified to the statement made by Seth on June 9, 1923, the day following the discovery of the bodies. The statement was concise:

S. O. Danner, being first duly sworn, deposes and says that he was acquainted with John Sprouse and his wife Florence Sprouse; that he last saw them at Garland Park, South Dakota, in the fall of 1919 or 1920; that soon thereafter I, together with my wife, left for Montana by automobile, and arrived in Gallatin County in November, 1920. I was driving a Ford and had a camp outfit with me. The first night in Gallatin County we camped in Rocky Canyon. The next night near Baker Creek, on the Yellowstone Trail, in Gallatin County. There I caught about 16 trout, and we camped there overnight. The next morning, we pulled out for Three Forks, and a couple of days later I went to work for Ed. Avery in Three Forks, driving the big city truck.

I make this statement of my own free will, with no promise from the County Attorney or Sheriff of any immunity, and I have read the statement and am willing that it may be used against me.

S.O. Danner.[57]

Peterson would also testify as to the second, more involved statement made by Seth. The court recessed while the date of this second statement was confirmed. It appears there was some confusion as to the timing of the two statements. Peterson indicated that the second statement, involving questions and answers, was taken in the private office of the sheriff, or, as Peterson described it, "that room just off from the public office over there, in the private office." For the first statement, there were only three persons present: County Attorney Peterson, Sheriff Smith and the jailer. During the second statement, there were more spectators, including a few deputies. Peterson was unable to remember how many witnessed that afternoon's questioning. Both statements had been taken to aid in the department's investigation of the case. Seth had been made aware that a stenographer, a Mr. Marvin, was in attendance, and that what he said could be used against him. Following Marvin's testimony, the statement made and signed by Seth that day was read aloud to the court. These early affidavits would be the only voice of Seth Danner at the trial.

Much of the questioning regarded Seth's relationship with the Sprouses. He was asked where they had met, what the couple had looked like and where he had last seen them. The latter he responded to by stating that he hadn't seen them since Garland Park, South Dakota. He was then questioned as to his arrival in the valley and his occupation and whereabouts since moving into the area. When asked what he knew about the bodies buried at Central Park, he stated: "I don't know anything about it. I couldn't say anything. I don't know a thing on earth about it."

Following this reading, Harland was returned to the stand, this time with the skulls in tow. One can't help but notice how dramatically the order of

Gallatin County Jail circa 1950. The sheriff's office was in the lower level, far right. *Gallatin Historical Society/Gallatin History Museum.*

events had played out. Due to Harland's "neglecting" to bring the skulls with him, Seth's words were instead read aloud, to be followed immediately with the brutal evidence of the crime he allegedly committed. The juxtaposition of Seth's words ("I don't know a thing on earth about it") and the showing of the skulls does seem to be what Rankin intended all along.

The woman's skull was placed into evidence as plaintiff's exhibit No. 4, then Dr. Charles Spencer Smith was called to the stand. Both Smith and a Dr. Elliot had examined the bodies days after discovery, but Elliot had passed away in the intervening months. Dr. Smith had been called on June 14 for the examination and quickly related how the bodies had been "badly disintegrated, but could easily be identified as to the sexes." His description of the couple matched that already given, and he was asked to confine his statements to the body of the woman.

It was noted that the woman's jaw received some sort of traumatism, a blow that had broken the upper jaw. It was not enough to have the skulls in the courtroom; Rankin requested that Smith present the skull to the jury. Rankin even asked Smith to "put the skull closer" and to "move along so that all may see." The doctor believed the blow, which could have been made by a hatchet, was significant enough to cause unconsciousness. It was not mentioned if the blow could have caused death.

In a comedy of sorts, when asked where the skull of the man was located, Smith replied, "I do not know where it is. Have you it here?" The skull was found in a box next to the witness stand. This poor show of professionalism of the courtroom was extended when Dr. Smith pulled up another bone from the box and stated, "this is something belonging to the woman, I guess." Rankin attempted to pull some statement about the dead man's trouser pockets from the doctor, but Dr. Smith could not recall anything being amiss. It is presumed that the mention of the pockets was to try to prove that a robbery had been committed. However, when one considers this "evidence," one can come to two conclusions. Either Sprouse had been killed for money, in which case the killer would empty the pockets. Or the pockets were emptied in a state of resignation. If Seth hadn't killed Sprouse but had to bury the bodies, and the situation had been a prolonged one, it seems plausible that Seth would think to empty the dead man's pockets. After all, what use could anything found in there be to the dead man, and what considerable use could it be to a man with a family living in a tent? But little more was said of this piece of evidence. In cross-examination by Mr. Smith, it was determined that Mrs. Sprouse did not have any of her real teeth; she had worn plates. This would be discussed again later, but the reason for this information coming to light was never really stated. It could have just been to identify the woman, but that seems to have already been fully established.

The atmosphere in the courtroom quickly changed when the next witness, Iva Danner, took the stand. The *Bozeman Courier* of the following day described Iva as looking "like a hunted deer"; while her former husband sat like a "human sphynx." It was noted that even when presented with Florence Sprouse's skull, Seth's "stoic demeanor and apparent lassitude" continued. The paper found his lack of "anger, resentment nor even interest," "one of the mystifying features of the interesting trial." Iva was applauded for her "herculean effort at self-repression" as she matter-of-factly told her story, though her body language seemed to indicate a fear of her husband. In particular, her testimony, "free from hysterical outbursts and mental confusion," was found to be remarkable, as most "murder trials in which a woman is the principal witness" were supposedly riddled with these emotions. If the paper told facts, it told them with finesse. Crowds were struggling to gain admission to the courtroom. Clearly, the publication had an eager-eared audience.[58]

First, the divorce was made clear to allow for Iva to testify freely of anything she had seen or heard. Iva's testimony was straightforward as she told of her early life and meeting the Sprouses. Her story followed that which had already been published multiple times in the local papers.

Iva testified as to her relationship with the defendant and was even asked if Seth had Indian blood in him, to which she responded, "yes." She was shown a map of the campsite at Central Park and asked many questions about the location of the tents as well as the life they lived there with the Sprouses. She detailed the morning and evening of November 14, 1920, stating where the children had been, including Florence Danner, the eldest. Florence had been in the tent with the other children, helping to get them ready for bed.

In the midst of Iva's testimony, the following interpolation occurred:

> THE COURT: Let us have order in the court room. Mr. Bailiff, do not let any other person in. We have too many here now.
> THE BAILIFF: Judge, I can't hold them back.
> THE COURT: Mr. Sheriff, you put a man out there to help the bailiff at the door. I have told the people time and time again that this old building is not safe for so many. Proceed.[59]

It's mentions like these that reminds one of the location in which this whole episode took place. In fact, it is this shocking contrast between what one thinks of Bozeman today and this vision of the Wild West or the Roaring Twenties that delights visitors at the Gallatin History Museum, the building that used to be the county jail—the very building where Seth Danner spent nearly a year. Judge Law was right in expressing concern about the courthouse building. It was fifty years old at the time, and at one point in the trial, an upper railing came dislodged, nearly causing a major accident on the stairway.[60]

In the courthouse of 1923, the trial quickly proceeded, as Iva continued her descriptions of what had happened to the Sprouses. Iva stated that, on the morning following the death of Florence Sprouse, Seth went out in the dark morning and came back in a short time. Then Seth asked Iva to make him breakfast. Later that morning, he asked Iva if she wanted to see "Jack" (John Sprouse). She said that she did and went into the tent, then quickly exited. According to Iva, John had a gunnysack over his head, blood on his

GALLATIN COUNTY COURT HOUSE AND JAIL
BOZEMAN MONT

Gallatin County Courthouse circa 1920. Note the neighboring jail to the left. *Gallatin Historical Society/Gallatin History Museum.*

collar, no boots and icicles on his clothes. She then spent the day inside the Danner tent with the children, keeping them inside, which was easy, since they had no shoes and the weather was cold. She mentioned the burning of the Sprouses' belongings and the selling of their car.

One interesting thing of note is her statement that Seth had killed the Sprouse dog with the ax. According to Seth's affidavit, John Sprouse had killed the dog earlier because it had fleas. Contradicting both of these statements and not mentioned at the trial was an article run by the *Bozeman Daily Chronicle* on June 10, 1923. The article states that the "Danners forgot one thing when they cleaned up the camp after the alleged murders at Central Park": an Airedale that belonged to the Sprouses.[61] It was noted that the dog had remained at the camp for days, unwilling to leave the area. A local family took to feeding the dog; when they moved to Livingston, they took the dog with them. Three very different stories.

Court was adjourned in the midst of Iva's testimony, as the hour was growing late. Her last statement was "he said he killed him for money." Following the day's trial proceedings, it was noted in the local paper that "not since the hanging of a Chinaman for the cruel cold-blooded murder of a fellow-countryman in a Tong war some years ago, has the people of Gallatin County evinced such intense interest in a criminal trial in this city."[62] The trial was being covered by the *Butte Miner*, an Associated Press man and by the *Bozeman Chronicle* and *Courier*. Again, one should note the immense interest in this trial and the way in which the papers could in many ways have previously had influence on those who were sitting in that jury box, regardless of what they may have said in their individual questioning. The subheading of this particular article in the *Bozeman Courier* was: "Accusing Witness Describes Details of the Most Horrible Crime Ever Recorded in the Criminal Annals of Gallatin County While the Spectators Sit Spellbound at the Dramatic Points Brought Out by Attorney Wellington D. Rankin—Danner Unaffected."[63] If that was as far as one read, imagine the images conjured up about the trial proceedings and the inherent sense of a guilty verdict that hadn't happened yet.

GRUELING CROSS EXAMINATION

The Murder Trial, Day 3, October 24, 1923

Long before the actual time of the opening of the court, the room was crowded and seats were at a premium. There were many women present, but their number was considerably thinned as the day wore on and the routine of the incessant questioning developed nothing particularly sensational or curiosity satisfying.
—Bozeman Courier, *October 24, 1923*

Court was resumed at 9:30 a.m. on the twenty-fourth with Iva on the stand. Rankin continued his questioning briefly before she was cross-examined by Attorney Smith. She again testified as to the details of her childhood and her relationship with Seth as well as the meeting of Florence and John Sprouse. Absurdly, Smith hounded her about the condition of Florence Sprouse's teeth, whether she had any or not. This intense questioning was never really explained and seemed to go on longer than was necessary.

During this long questioning, Smith attempted to reveal a relationship between Iva and John Sprouse that would credit Seth's insistence of her infidelity.

Q And when Sprouse was talking to you, did not Sprouse tell you, "I will dress you like a queen?"
A No, sir....
Q And didn't you ask Sprouse, "Where shall we go?"
A No, sir.

Q No. And Sprouse said to you, "Just as soon as Flo goes to town again?" Didn't
  Sprouse tell you that?...
Q And didn't you ask Sprouse, "Shall we take any of the children with us?"
A No, sir.
Q No. And didn't Sprouse say, "No, we don't want any kids in the way?"
A No, sir....
Q Now, about two days later...I will ask you if Mrs. Sprouse did not catch you
  and Sprouse in an act of sexual intercourse?
A No, sir....
Q And when Mrs. Sprouse caught you and Sprouse in this act of sexual intercourse,
  did not she tell you both that she would kill both of you?...
A No, sir.[64]

The questioning continued in this vein, with Iva repeating the same phrase, "No, sir," after each question and statement that Smith made. A discussion of what firearms both of the men had owned ensued, followed by another long string of "No, sir" as Smith discussed the day of the deaths. Rankin finally interrupted with an objection, to which the court admonished Smith: "I think, Mr. Smith, you are assuming the affirmative answer to the previous question." However, the same answer was repeated again and again. Smith questioned her about discussions between Seth and herself regarding going to the authorities about the deaths:

Q And did not you ask him this question, or say to him this, or something of
  similar import: "Will I have to tell what Mrs. Sprouse accused me of doing?
  And everything she called me and John?"
A. No, sir....
Q And did you not tell Danner this, or something of similar import, "I will kill
  myself before I'll go on the stand and swear to that, and you had just as well
  get that out of your head, because I'm not going to do it"?
A No, sir....
Q And when you talked with him about reporting this matter to the sheriff—which
  you say he did not—did not you tell him this: "I told you what we'd do, and
  if you don't do it, there will be three for you to account for instead of two?"
A No, sir.[65]

Again, the questioning continued until the noon recess, with almost all of Iva's answers being "No, sir." Following the recess, the questioning focused on a few rings of Florence Sprouse's that had been found among the Danners' belongings. When little could be determined there of note, the questioning turned back to Iva's early life, then flowed back into a discussion of what happened the day of the murders. When questioned about her original testimony of the murder day, nearly every answer was "Yes, sir" rather than the former "No, sir." She remained firm to the story she had related early on in the trial and even before that in her initial confession.

There was a brief mention of James Troglia ("Jim the Baker"), but little was made of it at that time. Smith attempted to pull out some mention of Iva's lovers, from different angles, but she adamantly declined the idea, and Smith could go no further.

Next to the stand was Mrs. Alpa Sprouse, the mother of the deceased John Sprouse, who identified some photographs and letters. She also testified as to her knowledge of John's plans when traveling to Montana. She could not remember the name of the family they would be traveling with but thought for sure it was "Danner." Her testimony was short, or rather cut short, as the next witness was anxious to head home.

H.A. Johnson was the county treasurer of Marshall County, South Dakota, and had perhaps the shortest testimony of all. He simply verified the serial number of the automobile that was purchased by the Sprouses in South Dakota and sold by the Danners at Three Forks. This was followed by the testimony of Jake De Boer, who had traded Seth a team of four horses, a set of harnesses, a wagon, a hay rack and a three-section harrow for the car, Sprouse's car. In July, the car was confiscated by the sheriff's department.

Deputy Sheriff Elmore was again placed on the stand to verify the car that had been brought in by its serial number, then was asked to verify the items that were taken from the Danner home during the investigation, including a shotgun and two rifles and a Luger automatic pistol. The rifles had been obtained by the department from James Troglia (along with a fishing tackle box), and the Lugar had been brought in from Pat Dougle. There was also a cigarette case, a Kodak camera, a box of various pictures, a hatchet and purses. These latter items had been found in a few trunks in the Danner home. Following the identification of the items, considerable time was spent in discussing exactly where each item had been found.

What ensued goes to show how the defense felt about the sworn statements made by Seth while in custody at the county jail. When introduced by Rankin, Attorney Smith objected, wanting to read through and check the information and its validity first. The conversation between the attorneys was awkward and led Rankin to dismiss the witness, G.E. Marvin, who had been brought to the stand to verify the document for identification as exhibit no. 23. Smith wished to have time to compare the document, presumably with the first statement that had been taken by Danner.

In the meantime, Marvin Sprouse, a brother of the deceased, was called to the stand. He was brought on to identify a knife that had been found in the Danner home. According to Marvin's testimony, he had received the knife from an English soldier in 1918 during World War I while serving in France. In the fall of 1919, Marvin had given the knife to his brother John. He would see John again in the fall of 1920, just before he headed out west, and he stated that John had the knife with him. He could definitively identify the knife by the strap, which Marvin had made himself. After Marvin identified his brother John in a number of photographs, his surviving brother Frank took the stand.

Frank also remembered seeing John just before he left for the West in the fall of 1920. Frank was asked to identify a cigarette case, which doubtless the crowd gathered in the courtroom already knew about. Earlier that summer, in July, it had been reported in detail the items that Frank had found in the Danner home. In particular was a unique cigarette case with the figure of a stork, which, when a spring was touched, would drop down into the case and bring up a cigarette in its bill. The box had been found in one trunk and the metal bird in another.[66] Frank had immediately recognized the case; there would be little mistaking such an interesting item. Many other items were also identified, including a shotgun that still had a scratch mark from a disassembly job that Frank had been a part of prior to John's heading west. Frank was also able to identify the knife Marvin had given to John; this time, it was mentioned that the knife had a can opener on one side. Frank also identified a hatchet that had been given to John as a gift for saving the life of a Native American who had nearly been killed by a backing train, along with some of John's handwriting. Photographs were again identified as to location, those in the photo and the time they were taken.

Frank had been an integral part of the investigation into his brother's death. In July, Frank, along with his wife and another couple from Firesteel, South Dakota, had traveled through Bozeman on their way to Yam Hill, Oregon. While in Bozeman, he had accompanied Sheriff Smith to the Danner home, where the identification of items had been made. It was his intention to investigate his brother's death in Oregon, where John had once worked at a garage, which was where, in fact, he had met his wife, Florence. The *Bozeman Daily Chronicle* noted that Mrs. Frank Sprouse believed that "John's wife's former husband's name was O'Hara, but could not tell his first name or anything further." As far as can be known, little was discovered in Oregon about Florence or the former husband of whom she had been afraid. This angle to the case would be little explored and, in light of Seth's testimony to come, was probably of no consequence. While both Iva and Seth acknowledged Florence's fear, neither pointed to this former husband as a killer in their final testimonies. Seth had used the idea as a red herring early on but had quickly dropped the insinuation. There was one other mention of a man named O'Hara in the *Chronicle*. According to the paper, the Luger automatic had been found in a Three Forks pawn shop. It was noted that "it had been pawned by a man named O'Hara, who said he got it from Sprouse when the latter was broke, and now he was in the same fix and wanted to get money for it. This was not explained further."[67] This second mention of a mysterious man named O'Hara is intriguing but, as mentioned before, must hold no bearing on the case, as both Iva and Seth made their stories clear. It seems unlikely there could have been a third explanation, like a jealous former husband, for the murders.

Next to the stand was C.E. Carlson, an attorney who had discussed the case with Seth on a few occasions, once during prosecuting attorney Peterson's

The first image of Seth Danner to appear in the newspapers. *Bozeman Courier,* July 11, 1923. *Gallatin Historical Society/Gallatin History Museum.*

absence in South Dakota when Seth had sent for him. In discussing the case, Carlson had attempted to form a more complete understanding of Seth's relationship with Iva. Originally, Seth had stated that there was no blood relationship between himself and Iva. However, Carlson had information to counter that, and when he related his findings to the jailed man, Seth stated, "Carlson, I see that you've got it."

This conversation on Seth's relationship continued with examination of J.E. Overholser, the brother of Seth's first wife, Alice, and the uncle of Iva Danner. According to Overholser, Iva and Seth had left under cover of darkness in 1916, and the family had heard nothing of them until they noticed in the paper this "alleged crime."[68] Most of his testimony revolved around verifying the relationship between Seth and Iva.

A Mr. Collet was called next to testify as to seeing and interacting with the party who had been camped at Central Park in the fall of 1920. Collet had been engaged in bridge work in the area during this time. Many photographs were shown him, to which he pointed out John Sprouse as the man he had seen at the campsite. He also had visited the camp more than once and had become acquainted with the two men, John and Seth. Following Collet, recess was called until 9:30 the next morning. Rankin believed that it would only take a half hour the following day to conclude the case for the state; however, judging by the amount of testimony given, it must have been much longer than a half hour. The *Bozeman Courier* reported that "Danner's complete testimony, both under direct and cross examination, will appear in full in next week's issue of The Courier."[69] This, however, would not come to pass.

UNANIMOUS FOR CONVICTION

The Murder Trial, Day 4, October 25, 1923

The defendant in this cause, Seth Orrin Danner, is accused by information of having on or about the 14ᵗʰ day of November 1920, willfully, unlawfully, feloniously, premeditatedly, deliberately, and with malice aforethought, murdered and killed one Florence Sprouse, a human being. Your verdict in this case must be either guilty of murder in the first degree or not guilty. Murder in the first degree is punishable by imprisonment for life in the State's prison, or death by hanging.[70]

The fourth and final day of testimony proved detrimental to Seth's case. Florence Danner was to take the stand, and all eyes were on the one person Seth believed could save him from the gallows. Prior to her appearance, however, Frank Sprouse was recalled. He was asked about his first interaction with Seth at the Gallatin County Jail, to which Frank related the following:

First when I went in, the minute he saw me he jumped up and said, "Hello, Sprouse," and stuck out his hand to shake hands with me. I told him, "You are the last man on earth I'd shake hands with." "Well," he says, "if you don't want to shake hands with me, you sure don't have to."…I asked him if he remembered what time it was when him and John left Mobridge to come west. He said—he studied a little while to fix the date in his mind, then he said, "I never saw John after he left Britton." I says, "You mean

*to tell me that you did not see him after you left Britton?" He said, "I do. I
never saw him after John left Britton."*[71]

When, at a later meeting, Frank questioned Seth about the Sprouse items
found in the Danner home, he asked Seth, "Don't you think you're going
to have an awful time to prove to the jury where you got this stuff? If you
didn't see my brother from the time he left Mobridge, where did you get it?"
To which Seth gave no reply, except to blame the situation on his wife, Iva.
It seems that Frank had tried hard to get Seth to slip up in his insistence that
he hadn't seen the Sprouses since South Dakota.

Following this, the statement from Seth that hadn't been introduced the
day before on objection from Attorney Smith was now brought again to the
court's attention. Smith allowed the document to be introduced but declared
that he did object to the manner in which it had been originally taken. An
argument ensued. It seems neither Rankin, the court, nor Mr. Carlson were
pleased with Smith's passive-aggressive attempts to proceed with the notion
that he was going to object to the circumstances in which the document
had been created. Despite this issue, the document was received and read
through in its entirety to the jury.

The statement had been taken at 10:15 a.m. on September 6 in the
Gallatin County Jail with County Attorney Peterson, Attorney Carlson,
Sheriff Smith, a Mr. Patterson and a Mr. Marvin present. The statement
was a contradiction to the very first Seth had given. He had dropped the ruse
that he hadn't seen the Sprouses since South Dakota and now seemed to be
telling his side of the story. It seems Seth believed they were interested in
figuring out how to best get the truth from Florence Danner. She was often
talked about in his statement. Seth began:

> *She seen the whole performance that the woman [Iva] and Mrs. Sprouse
> had. The woman hit Mrs. Sprouse with her ax. She is the gentleman that
> done it. And Florence seen it. I'd brought Florence in from the bridge up
> there above the camp. The two children come in ahead of me. I tried to
> holler to them, but I couldn't make them hear from the sound of the river.
> And Mrs. Sprouse come in the meantime and had this comflabertion with
> the Mrs. Mrs. Sprouse tried to kill her with this luger out here now. This
> luger, this pistol. She snapped it in her face, but it didn't fire. And when she
> threw the cartridge out, it didn't reload. The shell come right out and stuck.
> And then the Mrs. gets her. Bumped her off. That's the way it was. That's
> all there was to it. Florence seen her hit her. Seen it with her own eyes. And*

right there she commenced trying—commenced working on Florence, you understand. She told Florence never to mention Sprouse's name. If she did, she'd beat her to death.…Florence come to me and says, "Papa, what did mama and Mrs. Sprouse have a quarrel about?" "I don't know," I says. She says, "What did she hit Mrs. Sprouse for?" I says, "I don't know dear." She's asked me a hundred times why did mama not want her to mention Mrs. Sprouse's name.[72]

Seth went on to relate the row between the two women that he had refrained from telling to his young daughter Florence. He stated that Florence Sprouse had come to him enraged, telling him that she had caught Iva and John in the brush the evening before. She threatened to kill them both. According to Seth, however, she had already put in motion a plan for once the deed had been done: "Poison is what killed her. Poison she'd taken before she ever see the woman. Evidently enough to kill a horse.…When I put her in the bed—wife and I picked her up and put her in the bed—I turned around and there was a box open on the table…box of poison and it

Modern-day image of what appears to be a cleared camping area near Central Park. Author image taken almost exactly ninety-nine years to the day of the murders, November 17, 2019 (murders occurred on November 14, 1920). *Author photo.*

was open and two capsules were emptied, and she had dissolved it in a cup of water and there was pink powder around the top of the water line that had not dissolved, just as plain as the nose on your face....I'm satisfied she taken that poison before doing the job."[73]

Seth continued telling the story, this time backtracking to what he had seen as he had come into camp that day. He had seen Iva kneeling down, cutting up kindling for the fire when Mrs. Sprouse had approached her, gun in hand. When Iva saw the gun, she had reared back, exclaiming, "O my God, don't shoot." Concurrently as Seth saw what was about to occur, he shouted, "My God, woman, what are you trying to do?" By that time, Seth was close enough to make a run at Mrs. Sprouse, and she turned halfway around as he grabbed for the gun. Although Seth missed the gun, Iva was at hand with the ax she had been using, which she then used as a weapon to down the woman who had tried to kill her by hitting her on the right side of the head. Seth was still in a struggle for the gun as the woman fell. He detailed that episode as such: "She caught her hand in the works somewhere and tore her finger pretty near off. I held on—wouldn't let loose. She tried to work it by hand when she snapped it, you know. It reloads itself—automatic—and she caught her finger in the works in the back of it or in front, I don't know. She caught her finger, and I pretty near jerked the finger off when I tore it from her hands."[74]

Once the gun was safely out of her hand, Seth stopped Iva from continuing her attack. According to Seth, Mrs. Sprouse did not die instantly but later on, never regaining consciousness enough to know anything. In graphic terms, Seth described her death: "She died jerking just like a dog having a fit."[75]

Carlson then asked the whereabouts of Mr. Sprouse, to which Seth replied that he was down by the river, where he had been killed earlier by Florence, he guessed. It seems that Florence had told Iva of her husband's murder just before she had come after her with the gun. Nothing was done that night about Mr. Sprouse, however, as it was "darker than a dungeon by the time the woman died."[76] John had been easy to find the next morning, as Florence's tracks from the day before could be easily followed in the snow.

The intervening conversation between Seth and his wife was detailed by the jailed man:

> I told her that I was going to notify the authorities. She says, "No, you won't." I says, "Why not?" I says, "There ain't nothing to be scared about, mama." She says, "No, you won't." She says, "They'll stick me

County block 1 at the Sunset Hills Cemetery in Bozeman, Montana. The Sprouses are buried in unmarked graves amid the trees in the background. *Author photo.*

for killing her." "No," I says, "They won't. They can't do it," I says. "Florence seen what happened and I seen what happened, and you got all the evidence in the world." She says, "you'll never do it. I'll kill myself first. I'll never go on a stand on a case like this. Never. I'll die right here before I do it." I says, "Christ, now, woman, there's no use going crazy. We can't do nothing else. Got to. All the chance we got in the world." "I'll never do it," she says. And then she got hystericky and carried on.[77]

However, despite his being adamant about contacting authorities, it seems that he allowed Iva to sway his better judgment. The following night, the couple went out to retrieve the body of John Sprouse, which he covered with a sack, "so the Mrs. couldn't see it. She didn't want to see it."[78] Together, they carried it back and laid it in a grave alongside the body of Florence Sprouse. Prior to burial, a few items were removed from the dead, including three rings from Florence's hand and a watch and $1.85 from John's pockets.

Seth related the evening before the deaths, when everything had come to a head for the couple whose tent was nearly attached to their own. The Danners overheard a long argument between the Sprouses about the affair and what was to be done about it. It seems Florence could not be calmed, so Seth and John had discussed either earlier that evening or the next morning about their own plan. While John had little money, Seth had been willing to gift him enough to get on his way. They determined that they would split up and solve the issue of the women. If John really had only had $1.85 to his name, it seems unlikely that robbery could have been the alternative motive that was the basis of the case against Seth. The conversation, according to Seth, went as such:

> "John," I says, "I make a motion we just go and gather up our stuff and start in opposite directions as soon as we can. That's the only thing. We can't live together here, and I know it." I says, "This won't do at all." He says, "I don't know how in Hell I can. I ain't got but $1.85 to save me from death. The woman took the money, I guess she sent it to him." "John," I says, "as long as I got a dollar, you got a dollar. I got a little yet. I can help you some yet." "But I owe you so damned much now," he says, "I never can pay you. If you can stake me for money enough to get me to some town," he says, "where I can go to work, you just take my outfit." "No," I says, "I don't want it. I can't use it. I don't want it. I ain't got much money, but I'll divide up what I got...."[79]

He was asked to identify other items that they had kept from the Sprouses, which was nearly everything but their clothing. The one ring taken was probably worth about forty to forty-five dollars, he thought, but it seems that Iva had kept the ring, again dispelling the idea of murder for robbery. When asked about South Dakota and the trouble that Iva had gotten into, Seth reconfirmed his former wife's infidelity. He didn't comment on Kansas specifically but did state: "She's been keeping company with this little Italian down here a little over two years. Having wine parties with him. There ain't been a day in the summer season that he didn't spend from three to five hours out at my place."[80] He was quickly cut off from this train of thought and asked to relay a few more details about the death of Mr. Sprouse. It appears clarification was necessary, as Mr. Carlson exclaimed, "Oh, his own wife killed him?"[81] The evidence Seth used to determine this part of the story was what Florence had said to Iva before she pulled the gun and the tracks in the

Modern-day image of the road that leads down between the railroad and the old Yellowstone Trail. Most likely, this is the road into the Danners' campsite. Author image taken almost exactly ninety-nine years to the day of the murders, November 17, 2019. *Author photo.*

snow. There had only been one set of tracks in the snow out to where John had been killed: Florence's tracks.

Carlson then asked if Seth had resented the supposed relationship between Iva and John. Seth seemed resigned to his wife's behavior. He said he had talked to her about it, but it had been no use. He then added that the reason she had "trapped" him on "this right here" was that she was afraid that he would do it to her instead. The question was asked why he had thought this. He answered, "because she told me," then related a story that nearly four years earlier he had come home from threshing late at night and found the children home alone. He went to bed but set the alarm for 3:00 a.m., and when it went off, he sat up and waited for Iva to come home. When she did, the following exchange occurred:

> *I told her, I says, "Mama, that has got to be cut out. I can't put up with it. You leave the children alone and nobody to take care of them. Tain't right to me, tain't right to the children. If you're going to go this road, why don't you be a woman and get a divorce and quit? I'll give you the money to get it with. I'll give you one. If you want this son of a bitch, go with him. Don't be kidding me and the children. Let me have the children. You take this guy and go with him." She says, "I'll never do it. The first time you see me with him and get a little sore about it, you spill this other deal." I says, "Just what I'm going to do. If you don't do something. Just what I'm going to do. I'm just going to fess up the whole thing, if you don't come clean." Then she had another nutty spell, threatening to kill herself, and went through the whole rig-a-marole.*[82]

It seems this was a common occurrence, with Iva becoming more and more convinced that either her husband or Florence was going to tell someone about what had happened at Central Park. While she was afraid, she continued to spend more time away from home with the "Greek," as Seth now called him. He then went on to state that burying John had been like burying a brother. He intimated: "I never done anything in my life I was as ashamed of as that job, of putting them people away. I hated to do it. I didn't care about the woman. I could have done anything with her. But that man, it was just the same as putting my own brother in a hole in the ground. He told me when I separated from him and told him I'd split with him, 'Dan,' he says, 'you're too damned goodhearted. You can't live and do that.'"[83]

In two outbursts, he proclaimed: "I never in my whole God damned life, never killed a man. Never have. Never had an occasion to. There was no occasion for it at all….This is all a bull-shit scheme, every bit of it. That is all there is to it. It's a trap to catch me."[84] Seth also stated that Iva had continually ruined his life, and that at the time he had left Kansas during her time of need he had in fact left money and a down payment on a house behind.

There was little more to the statement beyond another reiteration of what had occurred that day at Central Park. His statement ended with: "I let her run loose too long. The people she's run with, there ain't a one of them that is responsible—not one of them."[85]

It was probably during this portion of the trial that the audience gathered there realized that Seth was not going to go on the stand in his own defense. This was the only statement they were going to hear from his mouth. The disappointment and maybe astonishment could be heard in the next day's paper, which headlined "Danner Will Not Go on Stand in His Own Behalf" before intimating what had been stated in his affidavit.

The reading of the transcript must have taken well over an hour or more. Following the reading, Rankin simply stated, "That is all," then called Mrs. Alpa Sprouse back to the stand to identify a photograph. When she was unable to do so adequately, Iva Danner was recalled and asked about many photographs. Once this was done, Sheriff Smith was recalled and Mr. Sprouse's watch was discussed. The watch had not been discovered until September, although it was known that Sprouse had had a watch. It was found on Seth himself, who at that time had been in jail with it for almost three months. When asked for the watch, Seth immediately told Sheriff Smith it was John Sprouse's watch but the casing was his own.

A recess was called, and then the most important witness was brought to the stand: Florence Dannner.

The paper stated it thusly the next morning: "The collapse of Florence Danner, the little frail piece of humanity upon whom both prosecution and defense in the murder trial…depended to solve the case, was the beginning of the end of the celebrated proceedings which have furnished many sensations during the past few months."[86] Both sides believed that Florence saw something or knew of something that had occurred at Central Park in 1920. At the time of the deaths of the Sprouses, Florence would have been seven years old, and she played a key part in the affidavit signed by Seth as to what had happened that day. She played no part in the testimony of Iva, although Florence was old enough that she may have gleaned something of the situation without actually seeing anything happen. In any event, there is no doubt that Florence must have had some knowledge one way or another as to what had happened that day.

The actual trial proceedings started off rocky. Attorney Smith objected to the presence of Mrs. Neely on the stand alongside the young Florence. The court immediately responded with a statement that the girl was in delicate health and it seemed proper to have a friendly face alongside her so that she wouldn't become afraid on the stand. Smith again objected but eventually gave in, as he must have realized that to fight such a request seemed callous.

Rankin began the questioning by asking the ten-year-old girl about their dog Sam, which he used to help her feel comfortable answering questions. He then asked about the journey west, receiving simple answers until the question was asked, "What became of the Sprouses?" The following was taken down in the transcript:

> *(The witness shook her head "no.")*
> *Q Do you know?*
> *A No.*
> *Q Did any one tell you where they went?*
> *(No answer. The witness is crying.)*
> *Q (After quite a pause.) How long did you camp down there, Florence? Do you remember how long?*
> *THE COURT: Gentlemen of the jury, the Court will be in recess until 1:30. During that time observe the admonition heretofore given you. Now, gentlemen, (addressing counsel) during the noon hour this little girl may regain her composure, and she may then tell what she knows about the case. During that time perhaps you can get together and talk to her in a way to find out what, if anything, she knows without putting her upon the witness stand....*[87]

However, Florence Danner was not placed back on the stand, and nothing was mentioned about any conversation during that lunch recess. It is unknown whether Florence was able to give any hint of what she might have known. If she had indeed seen what Seth had claimed she had, then Seth would have had little to worry about. But she hadn't said a word about it. Her silence in essence condemned the man, her father. It was Attorney Smith who objected to placing the girl back on the stand; he declared that he was not about to cross-examine the child. Florence was allowed to leave with Neely. Nothing had changed in the girl's reaction to the questioning. She had behaved in a similar manner each time she had previously been approached while in the care of the Deaconess Hospital. According to the *Chronicle*, when she had arrived in the courtroom, the little girl had "greeted him [Seth] with the happiest and sincerest of smiles," which visibly affected Seth. When court adjourned, Seth rushed to the child and embraced her. After talking for a bit, Iva joined them, and Seth "reached out his hand and clasped that of his divorced wife and the woman whose confession might send him to the gallows."[88]

Bertyl Linfield, a local photographer, was brought on to discuss the photographs he had taken of the crime scene on October 20, just days before the trial began. The discussion surrounded the vegetation found in the images, and the testimony seemed confusing. There seemed little point to introducing these images at this stage of the case, proclaimed Attorney Smith. Rankin had seriously misjudged the amount of time he would spend wrapping up his case on this day.

Pierce Elmore, Alpha Sprouse, Iva Danner and Sheriff Smith were all cross-examined by Attorney Smith that afternoon. Iva Danner's answers were again riddled with "No, sir" to many of Smith's questions about the belongings of the Sprouses. She said she knew little to nothing about the items that had turned up at the Danner home and more than once declared that her husband had brought them in to her seemingly at varying times. In one particular instance, Seth had brought her what appears to be exhibit 24, the stone hatchet, as a gift to end a quarrel. Iva stated that she had flung the item in a trunk without looking at it and later saw what it was and, having broken it, left it in the trunk. She had also received the cigarette holder as a gift from him, which Seth told her was a match holder that he had won on a punch board. She denied having anything to do with the gathering of the Sprouse items at Central Park and seemed rather confused as to where any of the items may have come from. Maybe she didn't want to seem like an accomplice to a scheme to rob the Sprouses of their belongings, but it does seem odd that she acted in this manner. It is also odd that she wouldn't have noticed a resemblance of the items Seth brought her to ones owned by the Sprouses if she was indeed not lying about them.

Following the cross-examination of Sheriff Smith, the state rested its case. A recess was called. Upon the return, Attorney Smith anticlimactically made the following statement: "At this time, may it please the Court, I desire to say that the defense has no witnesses to put on. We are going to rely entirely upon the statements of Danner that were introduced and taken before Mr. Carlson and Mr. Peterson. The only witnesses were Danner and the little girl.…Danner's story is all told in those statements that have been introduced by the State, and there is no use taking up the court's and the jury's time by going over it. Therefore, the defense rests."[89]

Twenty-five instructions were read to the jury, followed by the closing statements. According to the papers, "Oratory with all the sidelights of dramatic fervor, and passionate displays of conscientious effort opposed to a calm unruffled statement of conditions as they might have been, and with logic and reasoning to substantiate the claims, kept judge and jury, court attaches and members of the bar together with the audience, enthralled in a suppressed excitement throughout the entire proceedings."[90]

County Attorney Peterson spoke on behalf of the prosecution for an hour and fifteen minutes. In the next day's paper, part of his speech was published: "The individual who committed this monstrous crime…is no ordinary individual. In 50 years, this building has not been the scene of the trial of such an atrocious and brutal murder. In all the history of Montana, there is no crime which has a parallel.…This act perpetrated by this fiendish assassin was done in cruel deliberation and maliciousness.…What manner of man is Danner."[91]

The defense, as to be expected, painted a different picture:

> *The defense of Danner embraces four features: First, infidelity; second, Mrs. Sprouse finding out the intimacy between her husband and Mrs. Danner; third, the killing of John Sprouse by his wife; fourth, the killing of Mrs. Sprouse by Iva Danner. These four features constitute and make up Danner's defense.…In the presentation of this case, it is not only proper and necessary to consider the test—Danner's statement against that of his wife. There is nothing else to consider—his word against that of hers.… Iva Danner was what is called a good witness. Her simple story was direct and brief and to the point with no details. Keep that in mind—no details—and compare her story with Danner's.…If Mrs. Danner's story is true…then Danner committed one of the most gruesome crimes in the annals of the state.…If Danner's story is true, she has done what many have done since the beginning of time.[92]*

Attorney Smith went on to state that the motive of robbery "didn't square" unless the Ford car and the trinkets and "junk" were motive enough. He declared the real motive was infidelity. As pointed out by Smith, Seth had not been afraid of anything. Why else would he have moved only twenty miles away and kept a home for himself and his family? Smith noted: "He lived there longer than at any place since he started from

Justin Smith, defense attorney for Seth Danner, seated in the first row, third from the left. *Gallatin Historical Society/Gallatin History Museum.*

his home in Kansas in 1915. This fact is against all theories of criminology and the psychology of the criminal mind."[93] He ended his speech thus: "There are two questions to be determined in this trial. The first is, 'if Danner killed Mrs. Sprouse, he's guilty.' On the other side, 'if Mrs. Danner killed Mrs. Sprouse in self-defense, Danner is not guilty.' We have summed up our case and rest our fate with you."[94]

This was followed by a statement by Attorney General Rankin, undoubtedly a passionate speaker. As written in the paper: "When he became too severe in his tirade upon Danner, calling him at times 'a yellow dog; a dirty yellow beast as yellow as his face is now,' and 'a rapist; thief, bootlegger, and murderer,' Judge Law objected to the 'strong language,' and said it 'was unnecessary.'" In conclusion, Rankin demanded that the jury, if they fixed a penalty, must give no other verdict than death.[95] It was noted that his closing address was "one of the most forceful verbal indictments of an accused criminal ever heard in a murder trial in the state of Montana."[96]

The jury was dismissed soon after Rankin finished at about 4:30 p.m. It is interesting to note that both County Attorney Peterson and Attorney General Rankin spoke, bookending Defense Attorney Smith's statements. Given the strong language of both parties of the prosecution it seems unfair that both were allowed to speak for so long and that Smith was not given the last say in the matter at hand. Many probably would have forgotten Smith's persuasive speech in the light of Rankin's extreme language.

At 11:00 p.m., it was announced that a verdict had been reached. Within twenty minutes, the jurors were back in the courtroom. The verdict stated:

"We, the jury in the above entitled cause, find the defendant, Seth Orrin Danner, guilty of murder in the first degree as charged in the information, and fix his punishment at death. Signed. L.W. Watson, Foreman. Dated this 26th day of October, 1923."[97]

The jury had taken four ballots. It seems that never had there been a doubt as to the verdict of guilty. The many ballots were taken to determine the penalty. On the first ballot, there were nine for death; two wanted to leave it to the judge; and one voted life imprisonment. On the second ballot, ten were for death and the two remained who wanted to leave it to the judge. On the third, it was eleven to one. On the fourth, all agreed on death.

PART III

LIFE IN WAITING

DANNER STILL HOPEFUL

A Stay of Execution, October 1923–January 1924

There is no way that I can prove to the jury, or the people around here,
that I am innocent, so what is to be will have to be.
—*Seth Danner,* Bozeman Courier, *January 4, 1924*

Seth had been in bed at the county jail in the interim between the end of the trial and the reading of the verdict. The following day, the paper quoted him as exclaiming, "That's a hell of a note, to get a fellow out of bed at midnight to take him over there to tell him they're going to crack his neck…they might have sent that kind of word over without bothering me."[98] In fact, the headline of the paper read, "Danner Is Peeved When Disturbed to Listen to Verdict." It was noted that, following the verdict, Seth slept better than he had during the trial. It seems that throughout the ordeal his health had declined to the point that words like "feebleness" and "sick man" were used to describe his appearance in the courtroom. Within a day, and after a hearty breakfast, Seth was more like himself again, indifferent to his situation and hopeful that something would save him. He maintained that his former wife was a "dirty little liar" who had put him into this situation.

Judge Law would take a few days before pronouncing when the sentence of death was to be carried out. Following this formality, the sentence would have to be carried out not sooner than thirty days but not more than sixty from the announcement. This would give Seth's attorney thirty days to file affidavits and a motion for a new trial. When sentence was given that day, Seth was made to wait thirty minutes in the courtroom before being called to the bench. It was noted that "in answer to the question if he had anything to say why judgment should not be pronounced, the convicted man said nothing for an appreciable length of time, and the court had to repeat the question. Then, in a low voice that could not be heard ten feet away, even in the awful stillness of the occasion, he said, 'No, I don't think I have.'"[99] On the trip back from the courthouse, which required walking outside and down the sidewalk to the neighboring jail, the group, which included Seth, Undersheriff Orville Jones and Deputy Sheriff W.H. Patterson, had to walk through a crowd. The people gathered were awaiting a parade that would precede the annual football game between Montana State College and the State University. A number of uniformed officers belonging to the American Legion were present. When commented on by Seth, one of the officers escorting him exclaimed, "They're your firing squad." Seth smiled.[100]

Immediately, though, extra precautions were made to keep Seth safe until sentence could be passed. For the previous several weeks, Seth had been confined to the maximum-security area of the jail, or, as it is called today, "Siberia." Now he would not be allowed visitors, at least for a few days, and a death watch would be alert to his every movement. In fact, that following day, many women were turned away, all of whom said they wanted to "see Mr. Danner."[101] This strict formality seems to have been waived in a matter of days, however, as Seth repeatedly received guests in the ensuing weeks, according to the papers.

Iva, in hearing the verdict, was quoted: "It's too bad, but I had to do it. He's guilty, and he has it coming." She seemingly had no plans other than to get a job. Mr. Overholser, Iva's uncle, also had a statement to make on the verdict: "Danner's luck has failed him at last…the verdict was right. We always thought that would be his finish if he ever turned up—just this way. He was always lucky in getting out of serious scrapes. That has always been his record. But he was finally caught and will get what is coming to him."[102] Florence Danner was to continue to live with the Overholsers in Spokane, Washington, where it was presumed she had a good home and could attend school and live a somewhat normal life. According to Overholser, Florence had known nothing about Central Park, as the family had questioned her. However, since Mr. Overholser seemed set against Seth, it would be hard to determine if he would have permitted her to say anything she may have known to the contrary of his sentiments. The Overholser family did not take in the two boys Marvin and Donald Danner, and the whereabouts of Della Danner are unclear at this point.

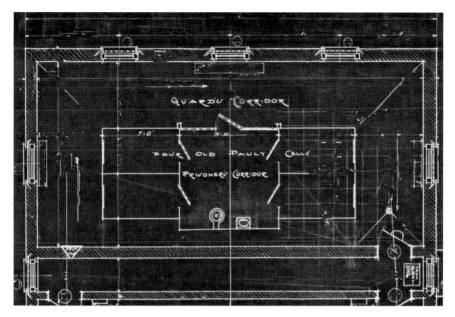

Original blueprint of the isolation cells, "Siberia," by building architect Fred Willson, 1910. *Gallatin Historical Society/Gallatin History Museum.*

One interesting thing to note was some of the details of what had happened during the jury's voting period. As noted in the paper: "At one time during the balloting in the jury room, one of the men who had voted for life imprisonment, explained that he did not want to put Sheriff Smith up against the proposition of hanging a man. This juror was so disturbed over the matter that inquiry was made of the official regarding his feelings in the matter. When it was learned that the sheriff had no scruples in carrying out the penalty of the law, the juror voted with the others."[103]

The relationship between the relatively new sheriff, Jim Smith, and Seth Danner was a unique one. There was an inherent respect, one that prompted Seth to say to the sheriff, "Well, Jim, they've picked out a hard job for you," to which the sheriff responded, "Oh, I don't know that it will be a particularly hard job for me."[104]

Following the trial, some items were taken by souvenir hunters from the exhibit table. Apparently, spectators had been allowed to come down and handle the items after the trial had been completed. The only thing of note taken was the inkstand and pen that had been used by Guy E. Marvin in taking down the proceedings in shorthand. The skulls were left unmolested by the "momento hunters," while many had longingly looked at the shotgun used to kill John Sprouse. Iva Danner had stayed after the trial to discuss the various items with her friends and others in the crowd. The sensationalism of the trial to the town of Bozeman cannot be denied. It was like a reality television show for those who became wrapped up in the drama.[105]

Now that the verdict of death had been passed, the newspapers could start to discuss the new drama about to unfold—that of an execution. As noted by the *Courier*, the jail, "like all the more modern jails," contained a built-in scaffold. This particular gallows, designed by architect Fred Willson, was built into the second-floor corridor of the building so that it became almost invisible along the railing of the balcony. However, once it was pointed out, one noticed the ring in the ceiling above the trap that would hold the noose. The trap had never been used other than in demonstrations by the contractors when the building was new, roughly ten years earlier. It was presumed that the department would test out the mechanism with a bag of sand to ensure that everything would go smoothly on the chosen day.

At one point, Seth had apparently alluded to the death of Harry Walker, who had been killed in 1920. His car and his body had been thrown into the Madison River; his head had also been covered in a gunnysack. It was a casual reference, but reporters quickly made a note of it, one paper believing that Seth would confess what he knew about that murder before his death at the gallows.[106]

While waiting for the date of the execution to be set, the newspapers continued to play up the sensationalism of the trial for as long as they could. The total cost of the trial, $1,581.33, was broken down for readers. Retaining

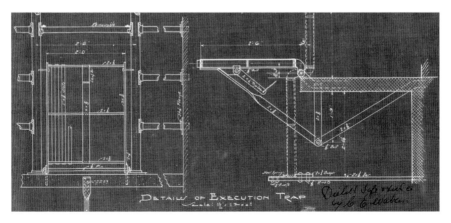

Original blueprint of the gallows mechanism by building architect Fred Willson, 1910. *Gallatin Historical Society/Gallatin History Museum.*

jurors had cost the most, $920.00, with meals costing $102.45. Witnesses had cost $458.88, and Attorney Smith had cost only $100.00, having been supplied by the county to defend Seth. This cost was considered extremely reasonable, as many had estimated the amount could be anywhere from $4,000.00 to 10,000.00.[107]

Sentence was not passed on the day it was supposed to, as Attorney Smith had asked for one more day to get documents together. In order to pass the time, the local paper reported as much as it could about Seth in the jail. It was noted that some local ladies had sent him little items like candy, cigarettes, magazines, books and "delicacies." It seems a female officer from the Salvation Army even brought in her guitar to be tuned, which he did "with a good grace, handling the instrument with skill and playing a few melodies before it was taken away from him." When asked about those who had condemned him, his words were extraordinarily profound: "I feel sorry for just 13 men…the 12 jurors and Sheriff Jim Smith. The jurors because they had to pass the death sentence, and Sheriff Jim 'cause he'll have to hang me."[108]

Already the papers had lost tabs of Iva Danner. Her original plan of getting a job locally hadn't been followed through, and it was thought she was planning instead to stay with her uncle, Mr. Overholser, in Spokane. She was supposed to visit her children at Twin Bridges before she left, but it was uncertain if she had. All that was known definitively was that she was gone. There would be little to report about Seth or Iva throughout the next month. When news came, however, it was of a shocking nature. On November 26, it was suddenly announced in a report from Butte, Montana, that Iva had married James Troglia that day. It seems she had spent about a week following the trial in Three Forks, where she spent a few "lurid days" before she traveled to Spokane. While there, Troglia had visited her, and an understanding must have come between them. Just a week prior to this announcement of marriage, Iva had secretly returned to Three Forks. The couple had chosen to travel to Butte for their wedding ceremony, which was performed at the courthouse with two witnesses: Thomas Fox, a deputy; and David O'Connor, a probation officer, both from Butte.

It could not be ignored that Seth had repeatedly stated that his predicament had been created to release his wife of his affections so she could go out with another man. It was noted that James "Jim the Baker" had long been a friend of Iva, helping to provide the family with food and clothing. He had been portrayed as the "Good Samaritan" during this time, all the while Seth pointing out what he saw as obvious. It appeared that Seth's view of the matter had been correct; he had never trusted the "Italian" or the "Greek," as he sometimes called him. The *Bozeman Courier* summed up the whole ordeal in one long sentence in the opening of the wedding announcement:

> *While her divorced husband, cousin and step-father, Seth Orrin Danner, an itinerant automobile mechanic of part Cherokee Indian blood, lies in the Gallatin county jail in Bozeman under sentence of death, awaiting the date of his execution, which was pronounced upon him last month by a jury in the district court, for one of the most cruel and cold-blooded murders recorded in the criminal annals of Montana, the killing of Mrs. Florence Sprouse, and her husband, John Sprouse, traveling and hunting companions of the Danners, on November 14, 1920, at Central Park, Mrs. Iva Bertha Danner, largely upon whose testimony her former husband was convicted, was married Monday in Butte to Jim Troglia, aged 36 years, of Three Forks, the man so frequently referred to throughout the Danner trail as "Jim, the baker."[109]*

This must be put down as one of the strangest wedding announcements in the history of wedding announcements. While many would have expected Seth to be remorseful over this news, the *Bozeman Daily Chronicle* seemed surprised to find that this was not the case. Both Seth and his attorney saw the marriage as an admission of guilt. Seth confirmed his feelings by stating: "I knew it would be alright…this man, Jim the baker, arranged all this thing months ago. All they wanted was to get rid of me and then they thought they would be safe.…It didn't surprise me much, although I didn't think either of them would have the nerve to do it so quick. I thought they would wait till I was out of the way. But they couldn't wait.…It just shows you that what I said about the killing of those people was true. I didn't do it, and she knows it."[110]

To bring his points home, Seth also talked about the time he had spent kneeling "at her bedside" praying "to God for hours to have her mend her ways, and be a good mother to our children." He related the many times Iva had apparently had affairs and how he had persuaded her to come back despite her insistence that she would kill herself if he ever said a word about Central Park to anyone. During the conversation, Seth had been seated on a couch in the isolation cells smoking a cigarette through a holder. When his attorney's cigar was finished, Seth handed him a new one through the bars, one that had been given to him, most likely by a woman in town. It also seems that James Troglia owed Seth money, about $140. According

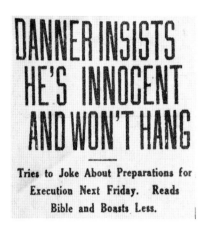

DANNER INSISTS HE'S INNOCENT AND WON'T HANG

Tries to Joke About Preparations for Execution Next Friday. Reads Bible and Boasts Less.

Newspaper headline, January 1924. *Gallatin Historical Society/Gallatin History Museum.*

to Seth, if Troglia had paid that money, then his family would not have needed additional help from the man through his humanitarian efforts. He again related his side of the story to the newspaper man before proclaiming: "I'll never go out onto that trap. I'm just as satisfied I won't stretch as I am getting out of here in a week....Faith and hope are great things. If you have faith and hope, you know it will turn out all right in the end. That is why I am satisfied I'll never stretch."[111]

It seems that a date had still not been set for Seth's execution and that Attorney Smith was preparing a document that would be submitted by early December for a retrial. One paper did announce the date of sentencing to be November 10, at which point Judge Law was supposed to have set the execution date. On December 12, it was announced that Law would hear motions for a new Danner trial. Affidavits had been gathered that Smith believed proved the jury had not been a fair and just one and that its members had prejudices against Seth prior to the trial. If the retrial was denied, Smith planned to send a petition to Governor Joseph M. Dixon, hoping to have Seth's sentence commuted to life imprisonment.[112] The papers seemed to believe that the petition would be a necessity and would stall the execution to some extent.

The five affidavits submitted to Judge Law were in reference to statements made by jurors W.J. Heaston, W.J. Booher and Burton Thompson. According to Earl Hinote, when asked about the trial, Heaston had told him: "If I was on the jury, I would hang him no matter what the evidence would be, for or against him." According to Hinote, Heaston's reasoning was that getting rid of Danner would be "getting rid of rubbish."[113] In response, County Attorney Peterson had entered counter-affidavits that cleared all of these men from contention. Interestingly, Heaston would end up in the Deer Lodge State Prison seventeen years later at the age of seventy-nine, having killed a man in a quarrel.

The jurors in the trial had been mostly farmers. It seems the court's delay in beginning the trial to allow for all to be present was not unfounded. Of the twelve men, nine were farmers; eleven of the men were listed as married.

Two of the men, Ralph Bates and W.J. Booher, were from Manhattan, and three of the men were from Bozeman: Leonard Hinson, E.H. Dean and L.W. Watson. Also called were Burton Thompson of Willow Creek, C.L. Watkins of Maudlow, A.B. Carter of Salesville, Ralph Newkirk of Belgrade, W.J. Heaston from Logan, A.F. Dawes of Trident and E.C. Watwood from Reese Creek.

Despite all attempts by Smith, Judge Law denied the motion for a new trial. It appears that Section 11962 of the penal code stated that no juror could be barred from serving, even if he had formed earlier opinions based on news or rumors, as long as he solemnly swore under oath that he was willing to give the defendant a fair and impartial listening. Another issue brought up by Smith was the residence of Booher. It seems he had only just moved back to Gallatin County and was actually a resident of Broadwater County at the time of the trial. Law clearly did not see this as a major issue, ending his statement thus in court that day:

> *After a thorough consideration of all the facts and the matters alleged for a new trial in this case, I am convinced that there exists no error of law prejudicial to the defendant's rights. And end must be brought to litigation always. The granting of a new trial in this case can serve in my judgment no other purpose than to permit the defendant to gamble upon another jury's bringing in another verdict, one possibly limiting the penalty to life imprisonment. The defendant has open to him for this purpose an appeal to the chief executive of the state if he desires to invoke such remedy. Certainly, there being no error of law, it will be unworthy of the court on the evidence in this case to submit the cause to the jury at great public expense and inconvenience and agitation such as naturally is excited by a case of this kind.*[114]

Following this dismissal of a retrial, Judge Law finally set a date for the sentence to be carried out. The execution date was set for Friday, January 11, 1924. Neither Seth nor his attorney had been in the courtroom that day. It was most likely assumed by many that Smith would appeal to the Montana Supreme Court for a commutation of the sentence from death to life imprisonment.

Once the date was set, it was ordered that a death watch be instated at the cell of Seth Danner from then until the sentence was carried out. While the men often relieved one another from duty, S.G. Bragg was most often the man who lived outside of Seth's cell. From this point through January, the newspapers reported different findings, at one point announcing "Danner Still Hopeful" and the next stating "Danner Seems to Be Losing Nerve." When relating his hopefulness, it was noted that his seeming indifference to his situation could be accounted for by his Cherokee blood. According to Bragg, Danner seemed to be the model prisoner. Among the officials, it was believed that he would never confess anything about the murders, and if he did, it would only be at the moment right before his walk to the death chamber or on the trap.[115] It was now a mere week from the date of execution. Two days later, the same paper reported a very different image of the man. The *Bozeman Courier* noted that Seth had lost his air of confidence and seemed to shun visitors to his cell, whereas before he would greet all heartily. While bidding a last farewell to some local women who had taken a humanitarian interest in Seth, he stated: "I've always had faith and hope... but as the time draws near the thought of it nearly has me down. There is no way that I can prove to the jury, or the people around here, that I am innocent, so what is to be will have to be. I know I have not committed any crime, or did any wrong that would make me fear my God, so I am not afraid to go. There is so little in this life, anyway, that things can't be any worse in the next life than they are here. Be good girls, and do the right thing, and I will meet you all in Heaven."[116]

According to the paper, even the jailer had to look away to hide his tears; the women's eyes welled at this final goodbye. It was noted that the secluded cell seemed "more like a mausoleum than a place of human habitation."[117]

As the day grew closer to execution, reports also discussed the preparations that were being made on the gallows mechanism itself. This work did not seem to be withheld from Seth, as he occasionally joked about the preparations being made to "stretch his neck."[118] It seems the balcony had been strengthened and a new ring placed in the ceiling to hold the rope. The original ring had never been used, and the switch was probably made to ensure it could hold the weight of the man who was possibly larger than what it had been designed for. It was remembered how only seventeen years earlier, in 1906, the hanging of Lu Sing had been botched by the executioners. On that occasion, the sandbag used as a counterweight had not been heavy enough and so had not broken the man's neck as intended but instead led to a slow suffocation of the condemned. Granted, the type of gallows used in this instance had been of a sling variety, in which a sandbag acted as a counterweight to basically jerk the condemned up quickly from the ground, breaking the neck. Clearly, the department did not want another incident like that to take place. It also seems that during this last stint in the

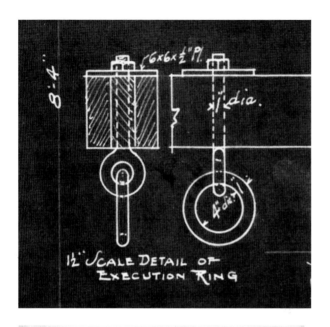

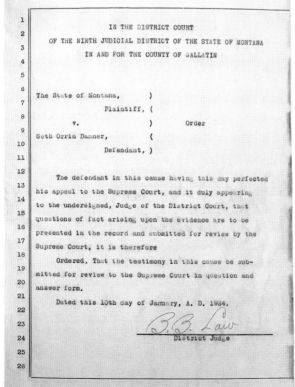

Top: Original blueprint of the gallows ring by building architect Fred Willson, 1910. *Gallatin Historical Society/Gallatin History Museum.*

Bottom: Inside of original transcript of the *State of Montana v. Seth Orrin Danner*, 1924. *Gallatin Historical Society/Gallatin History Museum.*

jail, Seth had put on weight, or as the newspaper decidedly announced, he had "grown fat." The hanging had to occur sometime between midnight on Thursday night and midnight on Friday night, according to the warrant made. The exact time would be unknown to those not directly related to the event itself. This was done mostly to keep spectators from crowding the building at the time the execution was to occur, regardless of their being allowed inside of the room. Only the necessary twelve men, doctors and ministers could be present, along with any immediate family members who wished to be there (of whom Seth had none step forward). As of the day prior to the event, the invitations had not been delivered, so as to keep the situation as quiet as possible. It may also be that the sheriff's department had an inkling of what Attorney Smith had planned. With only a few days left, it was reported that Seth was still eating three hearty meals a day and had been, as he always had been, a "model prisoner."[119]

The 110,000-word transcript of the trial was being prepared to be sent to Helena. It included the "testimony in the case, the judgement roll of the district court, affidavits and counter affidavits in support of a motion for a new trial in the district court" and the testimony of the accused jurors. Just one day prior to the execution date, the clerk of the district court, W.L. Hays, called Sheriff Smith, informing him that a notice of appeal had been filed to the supreme court of Montana by Attorney Smith. This immediately put a stop to plans and granted Seth a stay of execution. It was presumed that nothing would be decided until at least May. Seth would have at least five more months to live, to which he smiled and exclaimed, "A lot of people around here are going to be disappointed, for there'll be no stretching party Friday."[120]

EATING AND SLEEPING WELL

Life in Jail, January–June 1924

He likes to talk with his guards and often refers to his many fishing and hunting
trips and his various escapades during his life of vicarious wanderings about
the country in an automobile.
—Bozeman Daily Chronicle, *July 10, 1924*

Many who had been keeping tabs on the Danner trial through the
newspapers and general gossip knew there was a chance that the case
would end up in the supreme court of Montana and that Seth would not hang
that Friday. However, it had nearly come down to the eleventh hour.

The local paper quickly caught wind of an inconsistency with the stay
of execution. The *Bozeman Courier* claimed that Seth had known in the days
prior to his execution that his attorney was going to file this appeal to the
supreme court and that with the filing, the sentence would be stopped for
the time being. If he truly knew, as the paper says, then the newspapers are
not unfounded in stating that he could lose the sympathy of friends who
had bade him goodbye in those last days. He may have been playing up
the drama, like the farewell to the humanitarian women who he had all in
tears, as a joke. The paper apparently had information from some of the jail
officials, who stated:

> We have known all along that Danner has been trying to "kid" his well-
> meaning visitors....As soon, however, as the visitors left the cell room, and in
> fact before they had left the building, Danner would break out in uproarious

laughter and appeared to get a genuine "kick" out of what he considered the humorous situation of his visitors seriously praying and shedding tears in his behalf while he knew he was not going to hang on the expected date, and he was "fooling them" to that extent. After one of these Sunday visits when one of the officers asked him if he wasn't ashamed of himself for making fools out of those well-meaning people, he replied: "Ah, it won't hurt some of those old hens to shed a few tears. I knew I wasn't going to hang, but I thought I would have a little fun with them."[121]

While this seems an disingenuous way to be, what is one to say about a life spent cooped up in a jail for months with death hanging over one's head? Maybe one would be in the mind for having a bit of dark fun. At this point, Seth had been jailed for nearly eight months, spending a portion of that time in the isolation cells. The only times he had been allowed outside were in piloting the attorney over the crime scene and in his trips to and from the courthouse.

The Gallatin County Jail had been constructed in 1911, and the first of its prisoners arrived in December of that year. Almost immediately, there was a jailbreak. On the morning of December 22, 1911, all were surprised to find that six prisoners had escaped from the brand-new, $35,000 jail, which had been believed to be "escape proof."

The building had been designed with the neighboring courthouse as a key element. The boiler room of the courthouse heated the jail next door through the tunnel through which the first prisoners had made their escape. The area that held Seth Danner in isolation still has evidence of this heating system in small openings in the bottom corners of the cells where the heat could escape into the partitioned area. Today, without this heating in place, the room is usually a good ten to twenty degrees colder than the rest of the building, so it is hard to imagine what it would have been like for Seth. The cells have also been shifted about so that the configuration of the block looks vastly different than it would have been. The original blueprints are the only clue as to how Seth would have entered and exited the space for hearings and such. There is no shower in that area, so presumably he would have been escorted to the shower room on occasion. There was a sink and toilet combination that is still in place today. At one point, a couch was mentioned, so it is possible the department had taken pains to make the meager place more comfortable. By no means was the area supposed to hold a long-term resident.

At no time during the jail's existence did it hold such an important prisoner. Until this point, "Siberia" would have held only those who had

The isolation cells, "Siberia," at the Gallatin County Jail (later Museum). *Gallatin Historical Society/Gallatin History Museum.*

been deemed unruly or dangerous to others or themselves. Most likely, the mentally unstable had occupied the space before being sent along to Warm Springs, where the state mental hospital was located. In 1910, a man named Jesse Anderson may have stayed in that space, himself an escapee from Warm Springs who was caught wearing a suit of homemade armor and sent back to the hospital.

While Seth was under heavy surveillance, there was never a time when he seemed bent on escape. For the most part, he seemed content to live in the jail and socialize with his guards. In fact, the *Bozeman Daily Chronicle* reported, "Court officials say they are not worried that Danner might try to escape or that he will commit any rash act pending the carrying out of the death sentence."[122] During the Christmas season of 1923, he enjoyed a dinner "with all the heartiness and pleasure of a guest at a holiday feast," holding a conversation with his jailer. He often spent his time talking with whichever jailer was by his side at the time. Most often, the conversations revolved around religion, which apparently S.G. Bragg, who was assigned as the head jailer for Seth, found to be insincere.

When not talking to Bragg, Seth would often converse with officers of the Salvation Army about his religious learnings. His interest in the Bible was not new but did seem to become more important to him the closer the execution date came. While this interest never waned, on occasion, he had women to occupy his mind. Many in the community took an interest in him, most for humanitarian reasons, but a few as possibly something more. In particular, one woman was often mentioned, whether it be the same woman throughout is hard to say, as she remained anonymous. In May, she was first mentioned by the papers as a "young woman" who had "become interested in him."[123] Again in May, she was mentioned in reference to Seth's demeanor, although it seems her attention had lapsed: "For several weeks past Danner has been in excellent spirits. That was during the time he had a love affair on and new thoughts to occupy his mind. It is said his lady friend has not shown the enthusiasm of late that [her] seemingly deep passion would warrant, and as she has not been to visit him very often since the memorable birthday a few weeks ago, he has been left much to his own company."[124]

Seth's birthday had been celebrated by visitors and with a cake, complete with enough candles to number his years, forty-two.

Some guards took a keener interest in interacting with Seth than did others, but Seth had no trouble occupying his own time. It was noted by the *Bozeman Weekly Chronicle* that "when his guards show little interest in his stories, Danner amuses himself by walking about the cell, whistling tunes and taking his daily exercise of 'chinning' on the upper bars of his cell."[125] Prior to his being confined to the isolation cells in the fall of 1923, Seth had spent most of his time entertaining the other prisoners by singing, playing the banjo and showing off his strength. In fact, during those very early days

Seth Orrin Danner. Photo taken by Schlechten Studios at the Gallatin County Jail. *Photo courtesy Janet (Danner) Mann, granddaughter.*

in jail, when Iva was living in the women's cells, she could hear Seth sing and play, which was both familiar and a discomfort to her. She was known to send her banjo down to him to tune on occasion.[126] In the summer of 1924, his instrument (this time a guitar) was taken from him, as payments had not been made. It was returned to the dealer.

Early on in Seth's arraignment, his demeaner puzzled those around him. According to the *Chronicle*: "It does not matter what time of the day or night he is seen, not the least sign of distress or concern is shown by him as to the outcome of the charges against him. He is always ready to talk upon any subject, excepting the camping trip which ended in two deaths, and he laughs and jokes with his jailers and his attorney, when they talk with him. The nervousness which he shows at times is no more than the average man shows after weeks of idleness and the restraint of a cell."[127]

This confusion would be of endless interest to the papers throughout Seth's time in the jail. While he enjoyed having visitors, he did become perturbed when he was not given enough notice of them to get cleaned up. Of utmost important to Danner was his appearance. According to the papers, this was because his "bump of vanity" was "overdeveloped."[128] He was quoted as saying, "I don't care how many women come to see me...but I hate to look like a bum or hobo."[129] The women no doubt visited the man more often following the printing of his photo in the paper. As noted by the *Chronicle*: "He might be called a handsome man. Under circumstances wholly different, he would be admired. He might even be the recipient of scented notes and flowers and invitations. As a movie actor, he might be lionized."[130] One photograph, not seen in the papers, had been taken by Albert Schlechten. It was noted that when he was having trouble "getting the proper light on the prisoner's face, Danner said: 'It's hell to have so much trouble taking a fellow's picture, especially when it's going to be his last one.'"[131] In the photo seen opposite, Seth is well-groomed, with shined shoes and his guitar at hand.

This reference to his "bump of vanity" most likely stemmed from an interview with a local female phrenologist who happened to come to his cell one day. Seth was unaware of her intentions, so he was caught off guard by her abhorrence of his personality. After she left, Seth called her a witch and demanded that the woman never be allowed to visit him again. The woman's conclusions were published in the paper and were as follows:

> *Danner's head is very narrow at the dome. The measurement about the top is no more than his heavy neck. This shows the undevelopment of the prehistoric man or the degeneracy of the inbred Aztecs with their sloping and receding skulls. The protruding under eyebrows show a sly study of people, because his eyes cast down, as if looking through his brows. A deep cleft between the chin and lip with a rounded chin, indicates cruelty and weakness in principle.*
>
> *Another outstanding point are the very hairy arms, indicating great animal strength, and the very short thumb—the thumb of an ape, or a cannibal or an esquimo—which is often not developed beyond the first joint.*
>
> *The man's actions and his whole appearance and attitude give the impression of extreme vanity and extraordinary conceit. He delights to boast of things he can do and has done. He craves admiration, especially from women, and he has such faith in his irresistible qualities where the fair sex is concerned that his natural caution is lost. He will tell men many things, but he will tell a woman anything, even drawing upon his imagination to excite the emotions.*[132]

However, the publication of her findings seems to have done little to deter the women visitors who came out of humanitarianism, curiosity or genuine romantic interest. One of the women who visited Seth on what was to be one of his last days was interviewed by the *Courier*. She stated that, at first, she felt sympathy for the man when talking to him, but she quickly changed her mind when she reviewed the heinous facts of the case. In the end, she believed it was a shame he had only one life to give for those he had so "ruthless, so cowardly and so fiendishly snuffed out." Regardless of what people thought of him, interest continued to grow. Maybe it was the fact that the man "didn't crack" that led so many to want to view him. In any case, the newspapers continued from the initial arrest until the stay of execution in January to be completely enthralled with the man and his mannerisms.

Seth Orrin Danner. Photo taken by Schlechten Studios. *Gallatin Historical Society/Gallatin History Museum.*

It does seem that the woman's attempt to villainize the man by his appearance and brain was shared by others. It is a sad fact that in the 1920s there had been an attempt to implement the "Sterilization Bill," which would permit the government to sexually sterilize those it deemed to carry "bad genes." This included the mentally ill, incarcerated persons and at times those merely living in poverty. Much of the backing for the bill came from an economic and social standpoint. Many believed that in order to cut costs in large institutions such as asylums and jails, it would be wise to sterilize those currently in the system so that, should they return to the public, the spread of those genes would be impossible. A letter was sent to Franklin O. Smith, a professor at the State University in Missoula, Montana, in the department of psychology, by Governor Dixon asking for an examination of Seth. Smith refused, stating that he would not allow himself to get mixed up in a political game that would use his information as "propaganda for the passage of a sterilization bill." Smith did acknowledge the importance of psychological examination as a guide, believing that "if it should be shown that Mr. Danner is a low-grade moron, as Dr. Russell intimates, it might be seriously questioned whether capital punishment should be administered."[133]

One topic often discussed by the papers was his appetite. There is little doubt that anyone else had ever had such attention paid by the local papers to his or her habits of eating. There was endless curiosity, most often related to his appearance, about whether Seth was eating well and if his weight had declined or gained. When initially arrested, Seth weighed about two hundred pounds. Throughout the trial, he lost weight, due to some amount of stress, although he didn't show it in his manner. Most of the time, it was noticed with incredulity how well and how often the man ate, especially when things seemed most dire, when nearing the dates of execution. Following the guilty verdict, it was noted that Seth had eaten a hearty breakfast and had seemed to return to his normal self once the strain of the trial was over. In the weeks following, it was also mentioned that he was accustomed to eating three meals a day, while the other prisoners had only two. As the initial execution date drew near, it was noted that Seth had become so fat that his neck and face had the appearance of being bloated and the ends of his belt no longer met. It seems Seth had a real appreciation for the food he was given, in particular that which was made by Mrs. Smith, wife of the sheriff. Upon her return from the hospital, Seth proclaimed, "Gosh, I'm glad your missus is back…for now every tray will mean a good, square meal to me."[134]

While the jail was home to many prisoners over the decades, none would occupy the space for as long as Seth Danner did. The article that unveiled Seth's dark humor following his stay of execution in January was the last to report on him until May. It is possible that people had lost interest when they realized he had been joking around with his own death sentence. Or maybe something else had come up that garnered the public's attention. Either way, nothing was heard of him again until the case was put on the docket of the Montana Supreme Court.

Sheriff Jim Smith, in office from 1923 to 1927. *Gallatin Historical Society/Gallatin History Museum.*

IN BEHALF OF SETH DANNER

Letters to the Governor, January–July 1924

When I went to the jail to see my bro, I had to walk under that gallows. In my mind I can see him day or night hanging at the end of that rope. Gladly I would take his place if I could.
—*Mrs. Mabel Moody, letter to Governor Dixon, July 1, 1924*

Unknown to many involved with the trial—and possibly unknown to Seth himself—were the amount of letters sent on his behalf to Governor Dixon. While it is mentioned vaguely on numerous occasions that friends of Seth's were working on petitions to have his sentence commuted to life imprisonment, it is unclear if he knew the extent of those involved. In an age of letter-writing, it is important to note the significance of the written word. After all, the letters Seth had written to his wife, Iva, had been used against him during the divorce trial. They had even been published in the newspaper. This was not the only time the public heard the private communications of Seth. A letter he had written to his sister was published in December 1923. It was published with his permission, although it is clear that his allowance would have counted for little, given the history of the paper. An exploration of its contents helps to show how the man's printed words influenced others to write on his behalf. The letter, as published, reads as follows:

Bozeman, Mont., December 6, 1923
Mrs. E.E. Moody,

Dear Sister:—I received your letter this morning with the greatest pleasure in the world. I have wanted to write to you for some time, but was unable to get your address. Dear sister, but little did I think, when we parted from each other in Wellington, Kansas, a few years ago, that we would be brought together again by the means in which we were. You are the only living relative that I have heard of in seven years. I do not know where to write them. I heard a short time back that my oldest son Clyde was on his way out here and was killed near Carson, Colorado. I don't believe you ever saw him.

Well, sister, don't take any trouble to heart, for I have nothing to fear. You know that Jesus once said, "Fear not him that can kill the body, but after that hath no man power over you," for if God be for us, what men can be against us. If we live as God would have us live, we are not separated long and I would to God that you endeavor to meet me there.

You have no doubt heard the assertion made that I would give my interest in Heaven for this, for that or the other. But, nevertheless, I cannot recall having ever made such an assertion, but I do recall making that sacrifice. Seven or eight years ago I was living as near right with God as I knew how. I was prospering. I was living happy. I had everything I wanted that money could buy. I gave to charitable institutions. I gave to the cause of God, and it seemed to me that every dollar I gave that way, by some evening means, I received two dollars in exchange. I lived that life, thinking that I was living as God would have me live.

My home was broken up when God took my first wife away from me. My children scattered here, there and everywhere. Iva went to stay with one of her aunts, and it was only a short time until she told me she was in trouble, and begged me to get her away so that her folks would not learn of it, and I dropped everything and did what she asked me to do, and in 1915, in this state, at Dillon, I married her to save her reputation. She did not seem to have much love for me and was bitterly opposed to God and my way of living. I would get on my knees at her bedside and ask her to communicate with God. She made the remark that I was crazy, that I was talking to the wind—that there was no such thing as God.

But I took no heed of that, and I would thank God for the life He had spared me and the provisions He had made for me that day, and ask Him to watch over me through that night and to guide my footsteps the following day. And in the morning I would return thanks to God for the provisions He made upon my table for me and my family, and she would make light of me and tell my oldest daughter that daddy was going crazy.

And thus I went on living that kind of a life for some time, and at last quit communicating with God in her presence and began holding communications with God in secret, and I kept drifting away from God, and finally made up my mind that I had to give up one or the other, and therefore I made the great sacrifice. I gave my interest in Heaven and my love of God for a woman's love, and here about seven months ago, I realized what I had done. I discovered I had lost my interest in Heaven and my love of God and also the love of the woman for which I gave that sacrifice; and when I thought this over for awhile, I made up my mind to get reinstated with God, and I got down on my knees by the side of my bunk and began to search, and I made the greatest find that man ever made.

Man has searched this world over for gold and silver and has found it in abundance and in such quantities as to enable him to possess any worldly goods that his heart desired. But it will not buy what I found—peace with God. It will not pay for the sacrifice that God has made for man, nor the provisions He has made for him. God has prepared a new earth and a new Jerusalem through the prophet Isaiah, the Lord described the recreation of this earth to be the home of the saved.

(Then followed quotations from the Scripture.)

I would to God that my life might be spared, that I might be able to impart my feeling at heart and blessings of God that I have received, and also the knowledge from Him to others, that it might be the means of bringing their souls to God, and that by so doing, I might be partly able to pay my Father in Heaven for the great sacrifice He has made for me.

Well, sister, I hope that you will receive a benefit from this letter, and that you will impart it to others, that I may know that I have done some good in this world.

Please send a copy of this letter to sister Lucy and my love. I want you to help me pray for Iva, that she may not find any peace at heart until she gets on her knees and confesses the truth of this affair to God and the public, and asks God and me to forgive her. If she will do that, they will have to release me. How little her love must have been for me and her children to take my life and to give her children away as she did. It would be just the same as burying them to me.

I care not for the judgment the people have passed on me from the false evidence she has produced. God shall be my judge and He will also judge them that judged me and turned in that false evidence.

Well, sister, if we do not meet in this world again, may we live such a life that we may meet in the other, where sorrow nor pain cannot enter. Goodbye and God bless and keep you in my prayer.

From your loving brother in Christ,

S.O. Danner

P.S.—You were right; her man is a dago. If you will watch for the War Cry, published in San Francisco by the Salvation Army, you will get some of my writings. I do so wish that you could come to see me.[135]

It is very possible that Seth wrote the letter with every intention of its being published, allowing for a platform on which to declare his innocence and plead his deep spirituality and compassion for his wife and children. As far as can be ascertained, his writings were never published in the *War Cry*, but some were placed in the local papers in December 1923. Regardless, the religious strain would have no doubt influenced many to speak out on his behalf.

Holy Rosary Catholic Church in Bozeman, Montana, where Father Leitham, who often visited Seth, was based. *Gallatin Historical Society/Gallatin History Museum.*

In fact, it was just this part of his personality that many would reflect on in their letters to the governor. As expected, it was a common occurrence for someone who was religious to be against the death penalty and vice versa, so, regardless of how one felt about Seth's innocence or guilt, the end result is what they were after. One may also note in this letter to his sister the way in which the man writes. This is not the writing of a wholly uneducated man. Seth clearly was an avid reader and had probably picked up a lot of the religious sentiments from his talks with the Salvation Army, in particular, his reflections on trading in his salvation for the love of a woman. This may have been something discussed in one of the conversations with the local officers. In any event, many caught hold of his religion and grew interested in his predicament.

Seth's sisters' made up a majority of the letters. In total, five letters were still retained in the archives of the Montana Historical Society in the documents of Governor Dixon. Many more may have been written, but these are all that remain. Another four were from a Mrs. Lula B. King, who had read about Seth's story in the paper. The rest were divided among a few women, interested local parties and some religious leaders. In total, nineteen letters still exist, with fifteen responses from the governor's office accompanying them.

As expected, the most moving of the letters are those from Seth's two sisters. The first letter sent by Mrs. Mabel Moody was written on January 2, 1924, just a week before he was sentenced to be executed. After introducing herself as Seth's sister, she states: "If he is hung it will kill me. Him and I were pals when we were little."[136] She mentioned that she did not have the money to come and see him and asked the governor to commute the sentence to life so that she could see his face again someday. She received a response dated January 5 that let her know what many probably did not, that the case was going to be appealed to the supreme court. She did not write again until June, when Seth was again awaiting execution. At this time, she again appeals to the governor as Seth's sister, but this time she gives her opinion of Iva, mentioning her quick marriage and dismissal of her own children. She states that her sister, Lucy, had been sick all summer because of the case. The response she received this time was from the secretary to the governor, who merely acknowledged receipt of her letter; apparently, no other response was sent. Not mentioned in this letter, but mentioned in the next dated June 4, is the visit she had been able to make to her brother that February.

The *Bozeman Courier* had detailed the visit in a February 6 article. According to the paper, the two had spent a few days during visiting hours "laughing

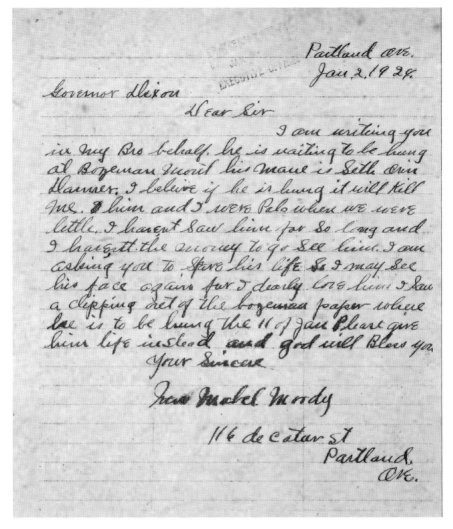

Letter from Mrs. Mabel Moody to Governor Dixon, January 2, 1924. *Montana Historical Society.*

and recalling incidents, humorous and otherwise" from their childhood on the farm together. Neither appeared to have the demeanor one would expect of a relative visiting a condemned man. It seems that Mabel had the same amount of faith and resilience that had been so puzzling to those watching Seth in the past year. It was also mentioned that she was the "very image of her brother," with dark hair, high cheekbones and sharp features seemingly indicative of their Cherokee heritage.[137]

Mabel's letter of July 1 mentions this visit in probably the most emotive words to be spoken about Seth. She states: "When I went to the jail to see my bro, I had to walk under that gallows. In my mind I can see him day or night hanging at the end of that rope. Gladly I would take his place if I could. Then I would not be left behind to worry and think endless nights and day if my brother has to go. I am praying to God to take me with him. We were pals in life I want to be his pal in death. Please Governor Dixon write and tell me that you will save my bro and God will bless you."[138]

In response, she received a letter again from the secretary to Governor Dixon stating that he was away on business for several days and would write when he returned.

On June 7, sister Lucy Marlow wrote her first letter to the governor in an appeal for Seth's life, mentioning their childhood together and how he had been the glue that kept the family together when they were young. Like her sister Mabel, she received only a response saying her letter had been received and would be brought to the attention of the governor. Her next letter was dated July 8. She had just received notice of his execution date and appears to have written immediately with her appeal for Seth's life: "O my God dear governor. Won't you stop it?"[139] She also states that his death will be her own. Again, she received the canned response that her letter had been received.

The sisters' letters each had a religious overtone, but neither discussed much about the case. They both seemed to find it incredulous that he could have committed such a crime, but it is unclear just how much they would have known about the trial proceedings and details of the case.

Much longer, more detailed letters would be sent by Mrs. Lula B. King of Mountain View, California. At first, her interest in the case seems vague. Her letters were peppered with religious fervor, and one finds it difficult to determine where one sentence ends and the next begins. Her stance seemed to be that of a woman against the death penalty, using the phrase "Thou Shalt Not Kill" multiple times among long quotes from Scripture. Finally, toward the end of her letter, she states: "Perhaps you are wondering what Seth Danner is to me. I answer 'nothing' and yet again 'Mercy' I never saw the man in my life. Never heard of him until I picked up a paper and read a short brief statement that he had been sentenced to hanging for murder. I felt moved with pity and wrote him sending him a little treat but that man's name has haunted me."[140]

In response, the governor (or his office) sent a letter also quoting Scripture, mainly Genesis 9:6: "Whose shedeth man's blood by man shall his blood be shed, for in the image of God made he man." Dixon stated that in his tenure he had commuted three men from death to life sentences, that he was not a bloodthirsty man but saw no doubt as to Seth being a cold-blooded murderer. Interestingly, this is prior to the appeal being sent him, although he was clearly well aware of the case. It seems that Dixon, possibly like some of the members of the jury who had convicted Seth, had formed opinions that were unlikely to be swayed.[141]

Lula King responded to this letter from Dixon by quoting the New Testament: "In as much as you did it unto one of the least of these ye did it unto me."[142] Either the governor did not respond or the letter was lost. Her next letter came on July 1, 1924, and brings up an entirely different point of view than any other that had been brought up in the case. It seems that she believed that Iva had killed Florence Sprouse in a rage over Florence having killed her lover, John Sprouse. While an affair between Iva and John had been insinuated during the trial, never had it been considered that Iva killed in rage. It had always been stated that if Seth hadn't killed Florence, then Iva did it out of self-defense, not rage. To illustrate her point, she states: "Now Governor Dixon I am a woman and I know women and I know that if I loved a man and some one killed him I might, nay more, I would be tempted to in turn kill the one that killed him. Of course I am not the kind of woman that would steal another woman's husband but If I were I would surely be the type that would avenge his death and in this respect women are all alike. I mean, when we love, we haven't any sense and our whole thought and existence center on the man. Ask your wife she ought to be able to explain this to your entire satisfaction."[143]

In this lengthy letter, very little Scripture is quoted, as though she thought a different tactic might sway the governor's mind. In response, the secretary to the governor wrote that, while Iva was not of strong character, it could not be disputed that Seth had "ruined her" as a child and there could be no doubt that he had deliberately committed the murders.[144] King was quick to respond that it seemed like the return letter she had received had been simply quoted text from a response that had been written to someone else's letter. She is correct, in that the typed page looks like an odd copy. She restated parts of the case that she must have read about in newspaper clippings and then bizarrely made her reply to the statement that Danner had ruined Iva by saying, "Danner has never mentioned this subject to me."[145] Apparently, Seth had written King a letter on January 9 in which he proclaimed his love for Iva. He gave King Iva's address, asking her to write to her to tell her (in the words of Mrs. King): "he loved her to the last and was glad to die for her and that his last wish was that she never confess the truth to anyone but

God and that he died praying God would give her that happiness for which she longed but had never had."[146] However, much like the letter to his sister Mabel, Seth must have known that such a letter was going to be read by the sheriff's department and maybe even printed in the paper. Knowing this makes it difficult to establish the sincerity of his letters.

In another bizarre statement, Mrs. King related the following information:

> *Seth Danner's sister went to see Mrs. Danner. That isn't her name now but anyway Danner's sister went to see her and that poor* [woman] *should put on her hat and coat twice to go and make a sworn confession of the whole story and her present husband stopped her. Told her that she would be hung herself if she did and would probably be mobbed before she had a trial. The poor woman walked the yard and house for hours saying she would go crazy if they hung Danner. She is at present in a sanitarium in Spokane, Wash, the Mother of a new babe. At least she was there expecting one when I last heard and almost crazy over the whole deal. Truly the way of the transgressor is hard, isn't it?*[147]

Where Mrs. King had received this information is completely unknown. There had been some rumor as to Iva being in a sanitarium of some sort. On July 15, 1924, Iva sent a letter to Attorney Peterson stating that she had never been in a hospital and hadn't been unwell at all since she had left Three Forks. The rumor must have also reached Iva, but it didn't seem to be published in any of the papers. King's information must have been false, but it would be nearly impossible to determine the truth of it. What is interesting is how King went from a woman interested in capital punishment to a woman who felt she knew all about the case, the family involved and Seth without having met a single one of them.

Lula King received a response from the governor with strongly opinionated language. He uses the words "preposterous" and "pure fabrication" in discussing Seth's statements about the murders and called the case the most brutal murder case he had ever dealt with.[148] There would be no more letters from Mrs. King.

Among the letters that were sent were two from Mrs. John H. Betz and possibly her husband as well. The reason for writing was to say that a fair trial could not have been had in a town that harbored so much prejudice against Seth Danner. Mrs. Betz believed that the "testimonies on both sides are only hear says to a certain extent as there was no witness to witness the crime but Mr. and Mrs. Danner."[149] Both of the letters written by Betz voiced a concern that a different solution to the case could be found, and that Seth could not be brought back to life if that should be the case. They argued for life imprisonment instead. The governor responded: "I would say that while personally I am not strong for capital punishment, at the same time, under the Montana law I am not justified in upsetting the verdict of the courts unless there has been an apparent miscarriage of justice…as the case is presented to me, from the record at this time I have no doubt that he deliberately killed the man and woman in cold blood."[150]

A similar letter came from a Chester P. Bales of Three Forks, Montana, who stated that while he didn't know the Danners personally, he believed that there was an issue with Iva as the only witness. Bales pointed out that many of the statements made by Seth had come true. While he doesn't state it outright, one could assume that he is talking about Seth's insistence that Iva had another man and the fact that she had indeed married quickly after the trial. The governor responded that the case was on appeal to the Supreme Court of Montana, and that would decide the matter. A Reverend Grandy from Great Falls also felt that the word of Iva could not necessarily be trusted and that, since she was the only witness, the case seemed to be

Jail bars in passageway between the bullpen and Siberia. *Author photo.*

lacking in truthfulness. It seems that Reverend Grandy had, as most people, considered the man guilty from the newspaper accounts and gossip but had since heard Seth's story and had even held a couple of interviews with Seth himself. While he didn't believe Seth was innocent, he couldn't say he was guilty, either, so imposing the death sentence could be a mistake. The governor's response was similar to those received by Mrs. King and Mrs. Betz. An interested party named W.F. from Spokane, Washington, also believed there was doubt in the case, as did Mrs. V.E. Metlen of Armstead, Montana. Metlen had written multiple letters, although not all of them still exist in the archives, insisting that Iva was the real murderer. Again, the governor responded the same.

Two of the most interesting letters to arrive were from Miss Anna B. Bilderback and Mrs. Mignor Quaw Lott, both of Bozeman. Bilderback clearly found issue with the character of Iva Danner, asserting the rumor that Iva was now lying in a hospital "losing her mind" over her guilt. It doesn't seem as though Bilderback necessarily found Seth innocent, but it does seem like she found it appalling that only Seth had been punished for what had happened and that Iva had been set free. She closes her letter as "a sister in Christ" and writes a postscript that she could start a petition against the hanging if Governor Dixon wished. No response has been saved.

The letter from Mignor Quaw Lott was on behalf of her sister Lucile Quaw, who was too ill to write. In the letter, she quoted what her sister wanted said, arguing: "He is nothing but a poor, sick child, with no more brain development than that of a child. Society has made him what he is and now society, with smug complacency, is punishing him by taking from him what they have no right to take—his life." Lott went on to reflect on the "hanging of a Chinaman" that had occurred seventeen years earlier: "I know what a fearful effect it has upon a community. At that time the gentlest people were temporarily transformed into bloodthirsty animals." Both of these arguments had not been voiced by anyone else who had written letters in behalf of Seth Danner. The governor's response was sent on July 24, 1924, and was the same canned response except for the first line, which read, "Unfortunately, your letter of some days ago relative to the Danner case did not come to my attention until today." It would have made little difference in changing the governor's mind; however, the word "unfortunately" is significant. Seth Danner had paid his sentence with his life only six days earlier.[151]

PART IV

DEATH OF SETH DANNER

SETH ORRIN DANNER TO DIE HERE FRIDAY

The Supreme Court Verdict, July 1924

If they think I'm going to tell them anything, they're mistaken; I'll walk up to the trap and get bumped off without giving them any satisfaction. I'll show them that I'm not afraid.
—*Seth Danner,* Bozeman Weekly Chronicle, *July 24, 1924*

Seth Danner was given a copy of the *Bozeman Daily Chronicle* that contained an article announcing the Supreme Court of Montana's decision on his case. It was said that he took a "hasty glance of the article, then turned to the apparent perusal of other news in the paper." This is how Seth would learn of the outcome and essentially the end of his life. The paper noted how quiet the man was that morning, completely different from his usual conversational self. Clearly, the news affected him.

Attorney Smith kept Seth informed of the proceedings of the appeal until the point of the actual decision. He told Seth that when he had traveled to Helena to state his argument before the Supreme Court of Montana, Attorney General Rankin had sure "ripped" Seth "up the back," to which Seth commented that he could "hear him from here." When Seth asked what could now be done, Smith was reported to say, "Nothing, we've shot our wad."[152]

The Supreme Court ruled that no miscarriage of justice had been found in the trying of Seth Danner in the Gallatin County Court and that the information relative to the possible incompetency of a juror did not validate grounds for a new trial. The official statement read: "Whereupon, on consideration, it is now hereby ordered and adjudged by this court that judgement of the court below, entered in this cause, November 27, 1923, be, and the same is, hereby affirmed."[153] Attorney Smith had had fifteen days following the decision of the court to enter a motion for a rehearing, but he declined to do so. Once those fifteen days passed, the decree was entered in the court records. Normally, an execution date was immediately set, but Judge Law was out of town, in Virginia, caring for his elderly father. The date was not set until the judge returned in early July, when it was announced it would be July 18, 1924.

On July 16, the warrant for Seth's execution was signed and read as follows:

> "To the Sheriff of Gallatin County, Montana, Greetings:
>
> "Whereas Seth Orrin Danner was duly convicted in the District Court of the Ninth Judicial District of the State of Montana, in and for the County of Gallatin, of the crime of murder in the first degree, and judgment having been pronounced against him on the 17th day of November, 1923, that he be punished by death to be inflicted by hanging the said Seth Orrin Danner by the neck until he is dead;
>
> "And whereas the said Seth Orrin Danner did appeal to the supreme court of the State of Montana from said judgment;
>
> "And whereas said appeal has been heard and disposed of by said supreme court of the State of Montana and the original judgment of conviction affirmed and the remitter from said supreme court having been returned to this court and filed here in on the 7th day of June, 1924, wherein the affirmation of said judgment of conviction is declared,
>
> "Now, therefore, this is to command you, the said sheriff of Gallatin county, to take and keep the said Seth Orrin Danner in your custody until Friday, July 18, 1924, on which day you shall inflict upon said defendant Seth Orrin Danner the punishment of death by hanging the said Seth Orrin Danner by the neck until he is dead; and these presents are and shall be your authority for the same. Herein and hereof fail not.
>
> "Witness, B.B. Law, judge of said district court, at the courthouse in the court room thereof, in said Gallatin county, State of Montana, this 22d day of June, A. D. 1924."[154]

The date of the warrant was set earlier than that of the signature, due to the fact that the judge had not been in town when the warrant was first made up. But it is unclear how the July 18 date was added, unless it

Judge Law in his Montana District Court office at the Gallatin County Courthouse, circa 1920. *Photo courtesy Dana Law Jr.*

had already been chosen and was just awaiting the judge's confirmation on his return.

Once again, the press took hold of the story, retelling the whole saga for those who had forgotten and detailing Seth's every move and mannerism. At nine days from the end date, it was noted that he ate meals heartily, whistled and sang, read the Bible and reminisced with the guards about his life traveling in an automobile. For a man who had spent his entire life in the open, it is remarkable that his health and attitude did not seem to suffer much as a result of the year of confinement. The guards believed "he is just the same Danner now as he was when entering the jail more than a year ago." Seth still seemed confident that "his luck" would pull him through. In fact, he was awaiting some money from back home (presumably Kansas) with which to buy back his guitar, which had been taken from him for a lack of payments made, and to help circulate a petition. To that end, he joked, "If it doesn't come soon, I won't need it."[155]

He also spent a considerable amount of time writing his sister about "The Tree of Life" of which she had asked him during her visit. He gladly wrote her thirty-two pages containing nearly five thousand words with numerous

LAW REGARDING EXECUTION.

In the matter of an execution, the law makes the following provisions:

The execution is to be held within the walls or yard of a jail.

The sheriff must be present, and must invite the presence of a physician, the county attorney, and at least 12 reputable citizens, and at the request of the defendant, permit such priests or ministers of the gospel, not exceeding two, as the defendant may name, or any other persons, relatives or friends, not to exceed five, to be present at the execution, together with such officers as he may think expedient to witness the execution.

But, no other person than those mentioned in this section can be present at the execution, nor can any person under age be allowed to witness the same.

After the execution, the sheriff must make a return on the death warrant, showing the time, mode, and manner in which it was executed.

"Law Regarding Executions," published in the *Bozeman Weekly Chronicle*, July 17, 1924. *Gallatin Historical Society/Gallatin History Museum.*

quotations from the Bible. His sister Mabel had been so impressed that she sent the writing back to one of Seth's friends in Bozeman who wished to get the document published.[156]

Contradicting the *Chronicle*'s take on the matter, the *Courier* reported that as the day grew closer, Seth became nervous and unsettled. The paper stated that "when apparently unwatched he runs his fingers up through his straight black hair, slaps his chest and knees and walks nervously up and down and back and forth in his cell in the manner of a caged wild beast who resents his incarceration."[157]

During this week before the execution, preparations were once again commenced on the gallows mechanism. The rope had been received from manufacturers, probably out of Texas. Almost immediately, the rope had been tested with a length of concrete culvert that weighed much more than Seth did to ensure nothing would go wrong.

Interestingly, this preparation did not seem to have been carried out prior to the January execution date. Surely they should have had a rope ready unless they were 100 percent sure that Seth would receive a stay of execution at that time. The law regarding execution was published in the *Chronicle*. According to the paper, no printed invitations would be issued, and it was not known exactly when the execution would take place on the eighteenth.

On July 17, just one day before the execution date, the *Chronicle* published a long article in which Seth was often quoted. The manner in which he spoke was deep and prophetic. When visited by a guest earlier in the week, Seth had apparently stated that he had never felt better in his life. Then he continued on in one of the longest statements ever made by the man and one of the last times he was given a platform on which to speak—the next platform would be at the gallows:

Why should you or any of the world pity me?...I am infinitely better off than any of you, for I know when I am to die and am fully prepared. You do not know when your end will come—it may be today, in a few hours or weeks or years. You are living in a certain atmosphere of safety, you believe, and you never think of death and therefore have made no preparation for the great adventure. It is different with me; I have known for months when I am to die and have prepared accordingly. My peace has been made with God and I fear nothing. I am happy and look forward with considerable pleasure to the end. I will go to the gallows with an open heart and free conscience, satisfied that the great mysteries of eternity are but a fraction of a second off.

The people I pity are the officers who have to bump me off. I feel sorry for them, for they have been good to me while I have been here and I know they are feeling pretty bad about it. I try to make it as easy as I can for them by telling them and in other ways show them that I am not worrying. But they look at me and think I am handing out a big bluff. They think I'll weaken when the time comes to step up to the works to get my neck stretched. But I won't, and they won't have to feed me anything to keep my nerve up either.[158]

In continuing his speech, one can see the influence that conversions with the Salvation Army, local priests and the like had on the man:

I have lived for 42 years…and by the way, the newspapers are much concerned over my age. I am 42 years old and have never had anything in my life worth living for. I have had to work hard ever since I was big enough and have never experienced much pleasure. During the 15 months I have been in jail here I have had a chance to consider the facts and look over my past life. From what I know of life, there is nothing very interesting or promising to look forward to. The world is in a state of turmoil. Read the papers any day and you will realize there is no peace anywhere on earth. Everything is upside down, and why should I desire to continue in it with the experience I have had and with no chance to better an earthly existence?[159]

This lengthy statement made by Seth would be reiterated on the platform just days later in a short and concise format just moments before the end.

13

NOTHING MORE TO SAY

The Execution of Seth Danner, July 1924

*It isn't a hard thing to die the way they have it fixed. It will only be a fraction of
a second before I'll be in another and better land.*
—*Seth Danner,* Bozeman Weekly Chronicle, *July 24, 1924*

Somehow news that the hanging was to occur sometime after midnight
on July 18 reached the local community. The sidewalks in front of the
jail following the dinner hour through the night were walked by those hoping
to catch a glimpse of the proceedings inside. However, no one was allowed
admission to the building besides those who had been personally invited.
They were listed in the paper days later as the following: Sheriff James
McClarty and deputy Clarence Gilbert of Park County, John S. Holland,
Thomas S. Kirk, John M. Arnold, L.E. Fuller, M.F. Getchell, David T.
Powell, A.B. Williams, M.B. Bond, T.L. Tillery, O.L. Devore, A.I. Poor
and W.E. Everson. Also in attendance were physician Dr. Joseph Piedalue,
County Attorney E.A. Peterson, priests Reverend A.D. Leitham of Bozeman
and Reverend Father Joseph Blaere of Livingston and Captain Fred Stevens
of the Bozeman Corps of the Salvation Army. Of the Gallatin County
Sheriff's Department were Sheriff James Smith, Undersheriff Orville Jones,
E. Max Howell, Roscoe C. Holland, Sil Bragg and D. Pierce Elmore.[160]

Those who were not directly involved in the proceedings of the execution
made an interesting group. Lafe E. Fuller worked mostly in the delivery
service, Martin Finley Getchell was a lumberman and at one point the
Gallatin County treasurer. Thomas Leroy Tillery, David T. Powell and Orin

Gallows platform
disengaged at the jail.
Author photo.

Leon Devore were all farmers. Myron Bernard Bond was a confectioner at
the time, Arthur B. Williams owned a barbershop and Arthur Illus "Shorty"
Poor was a grocery merchant. Thomas C. Kirk worked for a paper, and
John C. Holland was the law clerk. Why these particular men were asked to
witness the execution may never be known. None of them seem to be those
one would think would be called forth for such a duty. It is possible that these
men were chosen much like the men for the jury had been, called at random
as respectable local citizens to do their duty.

Priests Leitham and Blaere had the closest interactions with Seth during
that night. The priests had arrived at 1:30 a.m., immediately attending to
Seth in his cell at the back of the building. Less than an hour before his
death, Seth was baptized and made a private confession to the Catholic
faith. Whatever was said to the priests is unknown. Years later, an unrelated
local priest stated that Seth had been wronged, mentioning the confession
before Seth's death. He stated that those attending that night expected Seth

to confess to the crimes, but the opposite occurred. It is unknown what exactly constituted "opposite."

At 2:00 a.m., Undersheriff Orville Jones read the final death warrant to Seth in his cell. Seth listened quietly. Four minutes later, what would be known in the papers as the "death march" began. The procession was led by the two priests, followed by Seth, then Sheriff James Smith. According to the *Bozeman Courier*, "As he emerged from his cell, Danner was seen to smooth back his long, straight black hair with both hands and throwing his head back and extending his chest, walked with unfaltering steps through the long corridor, into the death chamber."[161]

The "death chamber" was located in the Jailer's Office, a very small room that sat between the Sheriff's Office and the Bullpen. The room measures about fifteen feet by nineteen feet, with a tight, awkward hall added to one side where food for the prisoners was passed through from the sheriff's kitchen to the jail. The rectangle of the room is further broken up by the concrete stairway and balcony that lead to the upper part of the jail, which contained rooms for the women and juvenile cells and the infirmary. A short narrow strip broke off from the main corridor that led out to the gallows platform. In this space, modifications had been made in preparation of this event. Two additional supports had been added that extended two platforms alongside that of the trapped one in the center, although it is unclear as to why they had been added, unless they were to support the curtain. The actual apparatus was covered from view by a black curtain, which had to be lifted to allow the men to enter the room and make their way to the staircase.

The stairway consisted of nineteen steps with two landings that allowed the trajectory of the stairs to turn from the east to the west. To make his way to the platform, Seth would travel under the gallows, then perpendicularly away from it, then parallel but still pulling away before the last two turns, one that would draw him back perpendicularly toward the platform and finally the last that would pull him in a direct line toward the mechanism. It would not be until that final turn that the rope would be easily in his line of sight. In many ways, this meandering path to his death echoes his meandering path through life. Throughout his year of incarceration, Seth lived in resignation to his situation and yet simultaneously in disbelief of his mortality. The walk away and toward the gallows mirrors his possible frame of mind.

What may have passed through Seth's head during that walk will never be known. Once, when talking to the guards, as he often did, Seth remarked that he wished they would "send him 'over to the big house for life' and then put him to work on the farm running one of the tractors at the prison,

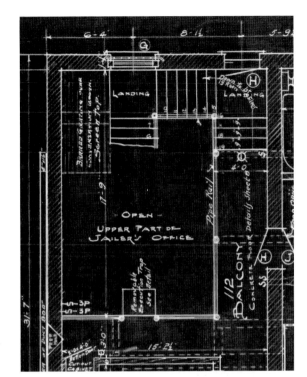

Right: Original blueprint of the jailer's office, "death chamber," by building architect Fred Willson, 1910. *Gallatin Historical Society/ Gallatin History Museum.*

Below: Upper level of the jailer's office, "death chamber." Note the platform and the rope to the right. *Author photo.*

adding 'I sure like to listen to the music of those tractors.'"[162] Maybe he was thinking of his life, what it had amounted to, or maybe he was focused on a new home where he could hear the hum of tractors. Maybe he believed what he had told the newspapers just days before, that there was nothing more to live for in this world and that he was ready to move on.

Once the group arrived at the top, Sil Bragg, who had been Seth's primary death watch guard, and Deputy Sheriff Howell positioned themselves on either side of the condemned man. Sheriff Smith attended to the adjusting of straps that were placed around Seth's ankles, knees, waist, arms and wrists. At this point, Seth was standing on the platform, for once the straps were in place it would have been impossible for the man to walk. Apparently, Seth watched Smith with interest as this job was done, and it was said that "not once during the entire procedure did Danner's eyes flinch or his demeanor show any signs of weakness or indecision."[163]

The priests read a Latin ritual during which Seth had held a small crucifix that he kissed before returning it to Father Leitham. It is unclear if the noose had been already loosely placed about his neck at this point, but it seems it was in place when Sheriff Smith asked the man whom he called Dan, "Have you got anything to say?"[164] To which Seth responded with his last words on earth: "I want to tell you people that I hold no malice against any man. I have made peace with my God and will go to Him knowing

Hood and rope used to execute Seth Danner in the Permanent Collection of the Gallatin History Museum. *Author photo.*

that I am fully prepared; and I would like to see each and every one of you people to follow my example. I have nothing more to say. Good bye, one and all."[165]

The black hood was then adjusted, during which it was said that many of the spectators turned their heads away. According to the *Courier*: "after a moment of silence the trap was sprung and Danner had fallen more than six feet into eternity."[166] If the curtain had remained in place, it seems that no one but those who were standing above the platform actually saw the body of Seth as it fell. It would then be on their word that the body had only had a "slight quiver of the torso muscles" before it swung motionless. Immediately, Dr. Piedalue checked for a pulse and found none for a minute. Four minutes later, when still none was found and no heartbeat could be heard with a stethoscope, Seth Orrin Danner was pronounced dead. In spite of this condition, Dr. Piedalue tried several times to find some vertebral dislocation but was unable to and, as such, determined the cause of death to be a rupture of the spinal cord at the base of the brain and in several places below. In graphic terms, the *Courier* stated that "both jugular veins had swollen to almost bursting proportions, and the cut of the rope extended under the chin from ear to ear." In many cases of hangings, the rope was left on the body when buried because it would have tightened to such an extent that it would be nearly impossible to remove. Whether this was the case for Seth or not is unknown. Dr. Piedalue and others later stated that it was "one of the most humane, as well as the most efficiently conducted hangings they had ever witnessed" in praise of the manner in which Sheriff Smith had conducted the whole affair. Following Seth's speech, the *Chronicle* noted that all had sighed relief, glad that the man had not broken down in that moment. "It made it easier for the men who were willing to see a human life snuffed out."[167]

The body was cut down after ten minutes, and it is unclear if the witnesses who had been invited in were allowed to see the body or if it had remained behind the black curtain. Captain Stevens and funeral director H.F. West (previously not mentioned among the spectators, so he may have been brought in after) placed the body in a black coffin, which was adorned by a silver plate inscribed with "At Rest" and a silver crucifix. At 3:00 a.m., the body was buried in an unmarked grave at the Brondell Catholic Cemetery, which was at that time north of Bozeman. (Today it is not as desolate of a place and not so remote of the city.)

The flashlight burial was attended to by Father Leitham and assisted by Father Blaere and at least one altar boy and was read in both Latin and English. According to the paper, it had been a calm and clear night, allowing the moon to cast its light upon the scene. By some reports, nearly twenty-three people were present, by others, only a few and mostly the officials. In one report, a woman was present, and it was noted that she intended to bring flowers the next day. It's possible this was the woman who had paid an interest in Seth during his incarceration, or it could have been one of the many humanitarian women who felt his death deserved some kind of acknowledgment. The *Courier* painted a vivid picture of Sheriff Smith in this place, relating that he had been the last of the officials to leave: "As he reached the moonlit road the soft, hollow thud of the hard, dry earth striking the casket as it lay deep in the grave could be plainly heard in the uncanny stillness of the early morning hour like an echo in the distance. The other cars had gone ahead and were lost to sight. He drove home alone, and in company only of his thoughts."[168]

Seth once said that it "isn't a hard thing to die the way they have it fixed. It will only be a fraction of a second before I'll be in another and better land."[169] While Smith must have been affected by the killing of a fellow man, especially a man he had become acquainted with over the past year, it doesn't seem like he had any scruples about carrying out the law. One must remember that this was Smith's first year as sheriff, and this had to be the most serious situation he was put in during his entire career in office. He was rarely, if ever, quoted in the papers, and he never seemed to talk about Seth Danner after the affair was over. Seth had indeed made the event easier on all those around him, just as he said he would. When one accounts for Seth's nomadic life, the officials he met in the jail would be the people, other than his family, that he spent the most time with in his life.

The official return on the death warrant, which was submitted early the next morning, read:

> *I, James Smith, Sheriff of the County of Gallatin, hereby certify that I received the hereunto attached death warrant on the 15th day of July, A.D. 1924, and executed the same, by hanging Seth Orrin Danner by the neck until he was dead, on the 18th day of July, A.D., 1924, at the hour of 2:19 a.m.*
>
> *James Smith, Sheriff*[170]

When one looks at the composure of his final speech, which, when given, had become halting, like someone who had suddenly been overcome with stage fright, one can only see an extreme measure of courage in the face of death. It is interesting, then, to note how both the *Bozeman Weekly Chronicle* and the *Bozeman Courier* saw this speech as an "admission of guilt." Since Seth did not declare his innocence, he must have been guilty. This was the same sentiment given of him when he did not take the stand on his own behalf. There is no possibility as to Seth having believed in his "luck" anymore, at the point of standing on the platform. It could be that Seth hadn't made a final confession to the public because, possibly, there had been no confession to make.

THE GOOD THAT HAS COME FROM IT

The Aftermath, July 1924–Present

No doubt the findings of the jury were correct, and the man richly deserved his punishment for a peculiarly brutal crime. But many people were left with an uncomfortable feeling that his story as presented in court was the true account of the killings at the Central Park camp.
—True Detective Magazine, *1935*

Printed in the back of the same newspaper issue that detailed the execution of Seth Danner was a much smaller article about a man named Charles White. The paper had reported in the Danner story that only two men had been incarcerated the night Seth was killed. However, this was proved to be untrue. There were two men—Tony Schwemmer, who had been convicted of poaching, and Harvey Walton, "a colored man" who was in for writing bad checks. But there had also been a third man, Charles White, who had been brought in on Thursday night, the day before Seth's execution. White had been picked up in Manhattan and booked as "crazy." With the department tense about the upcoming execution and the isolation cells unusable because they were occupied by Seth Danner, the man was placed in a pre-sentencing cell. Almost immediately after arriving, the man requested a doctor, saying that he had pains in his head and that he needed an operation immediately. A doctor was called for, probably mostly so that the department could remain in peace. Nothing could be done for the man, who was deemed by all to be insane. He remained in the cell he had been placed in without further considerations.[171]

Booking cells at the Gallatin County Jail (later Museum). *Author photo.*

On Friday night, the other prisoners knew what was to happen to Seth, and both were said to have "buried themselves deep in their bedding and under the cot mattresses."[172] If they had been watching, they probably could have seen Seth pass by on his way to the death chamber. Needless to say, the two men were unsettled by the events that were occurring. They were so unsettled that, when they heard odd noises coming from the cell of Charles White, whom they could not see, they said nothing. It wouldn't be until 6:00 a.m. Saturday morning, just four hours following the death of Seth Danner, that Charles White was found dead in his cell.[173]

There is a stark contrast between the quiet final moments of Seth and the torturous ones of Charles White. The bed in the cell had been soaked in blood where the man had tried to end his life by cutting his own throat. This hadn't accomplished the task, or maybe wouldn't have done it fast enough, so he then tied his belt around the bars at the top of his bed and dropped to his knees, essentially hanging himself. He had broken his own watch crystal to use the pieces as a knife. Both the watch and the belt should have been

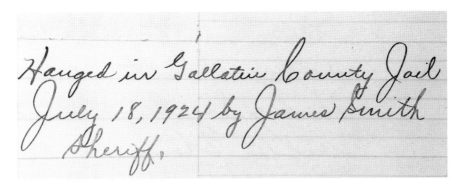

Return in original ledger book of prisoners for Seth Danner. *Gallatin Historical Society/Gallatin History Museum.*

taken from the man when he was booked as "crazy." It is probable that these two items had been overlooked due to the excitement of the pending execution of Seth. Dr. Piedalue was called back to examine the body at once. The doctor had probably never even gone to bed in the four hours between his duties at the jail. Little was ever known about White, other than the fact that he had been a laborer, was born in Butte and that his father resided in Plaines, Kansas.[174]

Accounts in the newspapers did not seem to chastise the department for its lack of responsibility in the matter. But one can clearly see the contradiction of a department that was praised for the humane execution of one man while another brutally ended his own life at nearly the same time.

It may be said that newspapers played a key role in the life of Seth Danner. It was the press that first brought the murders to the attention of the Gallatin Valley and the press that had been pointed at for giving people prejudices before the trial began. It was the newspapers that had detailed the life of the man during his time in jail, and it was a newspaper that brought Seth the grim news of his impending fate. It is important to note that the press was directly targeted by Judge Law in his denial of a retrial:

The newspaper is a daily necessity in the modern home. Its columns are perused in search of daily happenings…the world is eager for all the new. It may be said to be a matter of common knowledge and understanding that people do not accept as indubitably true all published statements concerning any happening or event. They recognize that at best it purports to be only facts as they are understood at the time of the publication, which must be verified before being worthy of acceptance as an established fact. Hence they are passed by the reader as current news and with an open mind as to the actual guilt or innocence of crime of the persons involved in the incident.... The laws of the state recognize these facts, and therefore do not exclude from jury service men who have intellectual ability to read and think and converse with their neighbors of matters surrounding the happening of any event or the commission of any alleged crime.[175]

Judge Law's words show a great confidence in the general public, maybe too much confidence. It is only in recent years that the talk of "fake news" has erupted. Was there truly an awareness among the people of 1923 of the bias of the news? However, without the press, little would have been known of the man unless one had been at the trial itself, which of course poses the question, how does one understand a man if the only source of information was believed by many to be skewed? This is the difficulty surrounding maybe every man's story. It is all just words, and in the instance of the Danner trial, it was his word against hers. One may never know the truth of what happened at Central Park or the man who died for those crimes, but some of the truth of the situation can be seen in those who lived because Seth had once been alive.

Ninety-five years after the death of Seth Danner, his life was considered by his great-grandson, Joe Stephens. Mr. Stephens is descended from Seth and Iva's son Marvin Eugene Danner, who had been sent to Twin Bridges with his brother Donald. At a young age, Marvin ran away from the orphanage, creating a life of his own. Later in life, Marvin would become a defining part of his grandsons' lives, in a large part due to the life he had been forced to live on account of Seth Danner. Mr. Stephens recalls that Marvin never talked about his early life, but that time spent with him was "by far the best times" of his life: "I never once heard him complain....There was almost no greater sin than waste....My Grandfather was the most caring, compassionate, giving person you could ever meet. He was hard as steel and soft as silk. He would give you the shirt off his back if you needed it but there was a definite distinction between need and want. If you had the ability to work and earn your own shirt but didn't, you could quite literally starve in the gutter and he wouldn't bat an eye but, if you truly needed help, anything he had was yours."[176]

Marvin was four years old when Seth died, but one can see the resemblance Marvin's character may have had to his father even if he hardly knew the man. However, the effect Seth had on Marvin's life is more profoundly seen in his absence. In clearly appreciative terms, Mr. Stephens went on to say:

Marvin Danner. *Photo courtesy Janet (Danner) Mann, granddaughter.*

The lessons my Grandfather learned came at great cost; they were hard, painful lessons but he took the absolutely horrid life he had and turned them into something great. I truly believe that if his life would have been easier, the life of every generation past would have been harder.

My life has been better because the actions of my Great Grandfather put my Grandfather in a very difficult position. As bad as the whole thing was, this is the good that has come from it.[177]

The somber positivity of Marvin Danner's life was lost on his younger brother Donald. The two probably never had a strong relationship of any kind, especially since Marvin had left the orphanage on his own. Some of Donald's life would be spent in the Deer Lodge Prison in Montana. At age twenty-five, he was convicted of raping a fourteen-year-old girl in Livingston, Montana, and was sentenced to sixteen years in prison. At this time, he was married to a woman ironically named Florence. His occupation was a mechanic, just like the father he hadn't known. He served only six years of that sentence but, within two years, was back at the prison, this time for forging checks. It is quite possible that he had come back to Bozeman asking about his father prior to his prison stint. Legend has it that a son came with questions, hanging around a few days before running off with a girl at an orphanage. Coincidently, the girl Donald went to prison for raping had just escaped an orphanage. Donald died at age fifty-eight in California, having been married to four different women over the course of his life.

Della Danner did not spend a lot of time at the orphanage. While it was never reported in the papers (probably because the excitement over the Danners had passed), it seems that Della had lived with her mother, now Iva Troglia, for years following the ordeal. She is listed at least through 1939 as living with the Troglias first in Spokane, Washington, then in Napa, California. Her first husband, Perry Curtis, was sent to the Montana State Prison on a charge of raping a fifteen-year-old girl in Anaconda. Her second husband doesn't appear to have lasted, either.

Florence Danner lived with the Overholsers for a short time. A photograph taken of Florence with her second husband, George Bacca, clearly shows the similarities with her father, Seth, in the high cheekbones and prominent brow. Florence died in 1965 at the age of fifty-two. Clyde, who Seth believed had died in Colorado, lived until the 1970s. It is unknown why Seth thought

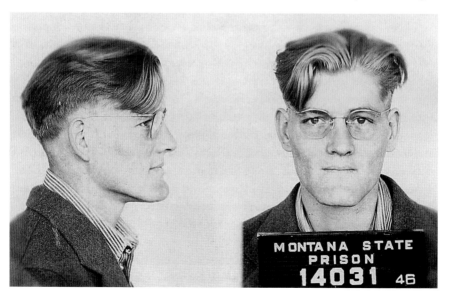

Donald Danner's prison intake photo dated March 9, 1946, at the Deer Lodge State Prison. *Montana Historical Society.*

his son had died. According to one family legend, Clyde and his brother Benjamin had attempted to attend Seth's execution but were detained along the way by the authorities.

Interestingly, little can be found about Iva following her marriage to James Troglia. She can be traced to California as far as the 1940s. And then she is lost. The date or age at which she died is unknown. It is possible that she married again later in her life. That may be why she is difficult to trace.

The week of the execution, Iva received a letter from Attorney Peterson, informing "Mrs. Troglia" of the plans for her former husband's death. Her reply arrived the morning before the execution and was delivered to Seth to read. In the response, she wrote: "Mr. Peterson, you can tell S.O. that I will meet him in Heaven; that we are all trying to go to the same place; that I hope that he don't do there what he has done on earth….P.S. Does S.O. ever speak of me?"[178] Seth had been disappointed by the letter; it seems he still cared for her, and it would appear that Iva, too, still held some fascination for the man she sent to his death.

A great-granddaughter of Seth stated that Iva confessed to the crimes for which Seth had been convicted and sentenced. According to her information, Iva stated that she had had an affair with John Sprouse, that Florence Sprouse had discovered it and, after killing her own husband, John, had come after Iva while she was washing clothes. Iva then killed Florence in self-defense. In Three Forks, Iva started an affair with Jim Troglia, and when Seth tried to send her out of his house, she turned in her story of the murders to the police. According to the granddaughter, Iva was paid $1,000 to testify against Seth under fear of prosecution if she did not. In a phone call to the Gallatin History Museum in 1991, the granddaughter related all of this as well as the following about a trip made by her aunt and uncle after Iva's death: "They talked with a woman at the courthouse and were given some copies of documents on the trial. The aunt and uncle placed these documents in an envelope and mailed them to themselves from Bozeman. The day they left Bozeman, they stopped out of town at a convenience store. Upon leaving the store, their mobile blew up, destroying everything inside. Because of this circumstance they cautioned [her] of inquiring into this matter personally."[179]

It is an extremely odd inference for an even stranger case. It is true that a sum of $1,000 was mentioned in a petition from County Attorney Peterson to the court. Peterson wished to ensure that his star witness stayed compelled to tell her story on the stand. He requested that she either be paid $1,000 to testify or that she be brought under the supervision of the sheriff's department so that, in either case, she would not or could not run away.[180]

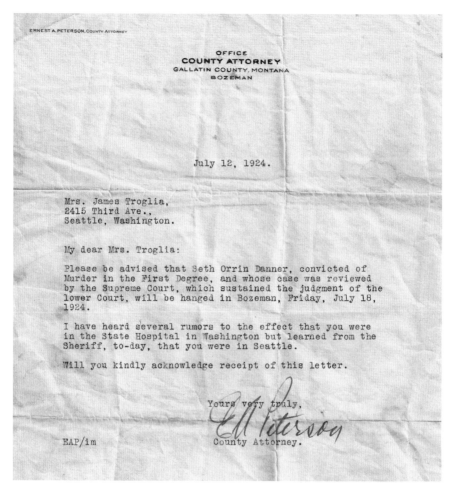

ERNEST A. PETERSON, COUNTY ATTORNEY

OFFICE
COUNTY ATTORNEY
GALLATIN COUNTY, MONTANA
BOZEMAN

July 12, 1924.

Mrs. James Troglia,
2415 Third Ave.,
Seattle, Washington.

My dear Mrs. Troglia:

Please be advised that Seth Orrin Danner, convicted of
Murder in the First Degree, and whose case was reviewed
by the Supreme Court, which sustained the judgment of the
lower Court, will be hanged in Bozeman, Friday, July 18,
1924.

I have heard several rumors to the effect that you were
in the State Hospital in Washington but learned from the
Sheriff, to-day, that you were in Seattle.

Will you kindly acknowledge receipt of this letter.

Yours very truly,

County Attorney.

EAP/im

Letter to Iva Troglia from Country Attorney Peterson announcing the execution date of
Seth Danner, dated July 12, 1924. *Gallatin Historical Society/Gallatin History Museum.*

According to altar boy Frank Seitz, who was ten years old when he
attended the 3:00 a.m. service the night of Seth's execution, he remembered
people saying that Danner was a "very large and strong man. So strong
that he could lift one end of a car to put the jack under it. He was also said
to be a kind man and not capable of doing harm to anyone, especially a
woman."[181] Judge Law's grandson Dana Law states: "Interestingly, many
years ago, my father told me that this trial bothered his father, the Judge. He
did not elaborate, and I didn't ask any questions. I supposed at the time that
it was the imposition of the death sentence, but it could have been the jury
verdict."[182] We will never know whether it was the fact that it was probably

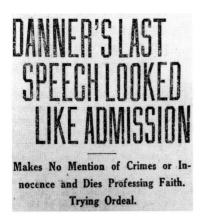

DANNER'S LAST SPEECH LOOKED LIKE ADMISSION

Makes No Mention of Crimes or Innocence and Dies Professing Faith. Trying Ordeal.

Newspaper headline, *Bozeman Weekly Chronicle*, July 24, 1924. *Gallatin Historical Society/Gallatin History Museum.*

the only death penalty sentence he had to pass or if something had been wrong about the outcome.

Fascination in this story lived on. A decade following Seth's death, the story was run in an article by M.M. Atwater in *True Detective Magazine* in July 1935. The finding of the bodies was reiterated for the much wider national audience that was now learning about the case for the first time. The article is in error quite a bit as to the proceedings of the trial, but a sentiment runs through that quite possibly the verdict was wrong. Iva's deathbed confession is mentioned here, which is of note, since Iva was still very much alive and living most likely in California at this time. According to the author, the moral of the story—as "every murder story holds a moral or a warning"—is "that those who set out on camping trips would be wise to know very thoroughly the quality and character of their traveling companions."[183]

The story continued to receive attention, most often at Halloween time throughout the valley, and it was often reiterated in the local paper. The writing of this book is the most intensive investigation that has gone into the case in nearly one hundred years. In conducting research, it was discovered that the gallows platform worked in a manner very differently than had been originally believed by historians of the 1980s. The rope to drop the platform would have been pulled upward at a forty-five-degree angle, meaning the hangman had either been standing right behind Seth or in the room directly behind, in the infirmary. Staff was able to debunk the legend that there had been three ropes run through a wall in the downstairs vault so that none would know who pulled the real rope. The dent in the wall many had believed to be the place where the ropes ran downward was found to actually be the kickback from the arm of the mechanism hitting the wall. When sprung, the clang was deafening as metal hit concrete. This is something not mentioned in the articles of the actual execution. However, attempts to uncover a mark in the wall directly behind the gallows have been unsuccessful; either a wonderful patch job has been done or it is possible the executioner stood right there behind

Modern-day image of the road that leads down between the railroad and the old Yellowstone trail. This is likely the road into the Danners' campsite. The photo was taken by the author ninety-six years to the day of the discovery of the bodies, June 8, 2019 (original discovery was on June 8, 1923). *Author photo.*

Seth but was, amazingly, never exposed in the press by those who were present.

For the first time, an exhibit has been dedicated to this story, titled *In Behalf of Seth Danner: A Crime, Trial and Execution.* The exhibit bombards visitors with the headlines and articles that chronicled the case while striving to bring out the question, in light of this contemporary commentary, did Seth Danner get a fair trial? The exhibit winds around the hall just under the gallows, where a faux rope has been hung in a noose.

Research on Seth's life and that of his offspring will continue and hopefully flourish as more of his descendants come to learn of his story. While attempts were made to interview more of Seth's descendents, most of the requests were either ignored or were never fulfilled after the initial contact. It is then with hope that this book is presented as a starting point for further discussion and reflection on his life and the continued impact of Seth Orrin Danner's death. With the only two witnesses to the crime long gone and those most connected with it also passed away, there are few if any who may know anything about what really happened on November 14, 1920, at Central Park, or if the man who paid his sentence on July 18, 1924, was indeed guilty.

NOTES

Chapter 1

1. "Danner's Last Speech Looked Like Admission," *Bozeman (MT) Weekly Chronicle*, July 24, 1924.
2. "'Not Guilty,' Danner's Plea to Murder Charges," *Bozeman (MT) Daily Chronicle*, June 12, 1923.
3. "Nancy Overholser Danner," obituary, *Plainsville (KS) Times*, November 18, 1915.
4. "Danner Worked in Dillon Was an Expert Machinist," *Dillon (MT) Examiner*, June 20, 1923.
5. "Two Murder Victims Are Identified," *Bozeman Daily Chronicle*, June 15, 1923.

Chapter 2

6. Court transcript, Danner Affidavit, page 40. Gallatin Historical Society, Bozeman, Montana.
7. Ibid.

Chapter 3

8. "Find Seagraves Not Guilty of Larceny Charge," *Bozeman Daily Chronicle*, July 19, 1923.
9. "Seagraves Will Be Given Trial on Wednesday," *Bozeman Daily Chronicle*, July 12, 1923.
10. "Conscience-Stricken Wife Tells of Husband's Brutal Murders," *Bozeman Daily Chronicle*, June 9, 1923.
11. Ibid.

12. "To Hold Inquest Over Victims of Pit Murders," *Bozeman Daily Chronicle*, June 13, 1923.

13. Ibid.

14. Ibid.

15. "Conscience-Stricken Wife Tells of Husband's Brutal Murders."

16. Court transcript, Iva Danner Testimony, page 86. Gallatin Historical Society.

17. Ibid., 89.

18. Ibid., 90.

19. Ibid., 91.

20. "Accused Slayer Still Maintains He Is Innocent," *Bozeman Daily Chronicle*, July 29, 1923.

21. "Conscience-Stricken Wife Tells of Husband's Brutal Murders."

22. "Slayer's Wife Tells Why She Revealed Crime," *Bozeman Daily Chronicle*, June 16, 1923.

23. "Danner Denies Wife's Grim Charge," *Bozeman Daily Chronicle*, June 10, 1923.

24. "'Not Guilty,' Danner's Plea to Murder Charges," *Bozeman Daily Chronicle*, June 12, 1923.

25. Ibid.

26. "Camp on Site of Double Murder—But Not for Long," *Bozeman Daily Chronicle*, June 10, 1923.

27. "What Moved Iva Danner to Confess Husband's Crimes?" *Bozeman Daily Chronicle*, June 10, 1923.

28. Ibid.

Chapter 4

29. "Danner Denies Wife's Grim Charge," *Bozeman Daily Chronicle*, June 10, 1923.

30. "Fear of Husband Not Conscience Led to Avowal," *Bozeman Daily Chronicle*, June 17, 1923.

31. "Danner Passed Scene of Crime Scores of Times," *Bozeman Daily Chronicle* June 19, 1923.

32. "Strategic Move to Save Danner Made by Lawyer," *Bozeman Daily Chronicle*, June 30, 1923.

33. "Danner Wins First Round in Divorce Fight," *Bozeman Daily Chronicle*, July 11, 1923.

34. "Danner Used Murder Axe as Household Tool," *Bozeman Daily Chronicle*, June 14, 1923.

35. "Danner Children Go to State Home," *Bozeman Daily Chronicle*, July 4, 1923.

36. "Danner Children Will Have a Good Home with Uncle," *Bozeman Daily Chronicle*, July 22, 1923.

37. Ibid.

38. "Danner Fights Divorce Action of Child Wife," *Bozeman Daily Chronicle*, August 17, 1923.

39. Ibid.

40. "Danner Divorce Case Attracts Large Audience," *Bozeman Daily Chronicle*, August 26, 1923.

41. Ibid.

42. Ibid.

43. Ibid.

44. Ibid.

45. "Mrs. Danner Is Granted Decree by Judge B. Law," *Bozeman Daily Chronicle*, August 29, 1923.

Chapter 5

46. "Danner Pilots Attorney Over Camping Ground," *Bozeman Daily Chronicle*, October 19, 1923.

47. Ibid.

48. Ibid.

49. "Danner Passed Scene of Crime Scores of Times," *Bozeman Daily Chronicle*, June 19, 1923.

50. Order, *The State of Montana vs. Seth Orin Danner*. District Court of the Ninth Judicial District of the State of Montana, July 2, 1923.

51. "Legal Talent Alert for Surprises When Danner Case Begins," *Bozeman Daily Chronicle*, October 1923.

52. Ibid.

53. Ibid.

54. Ibid.

55. "Frank Sprouse Helping in the Murder Search," *Bozeman Daily Chronicle*, July 7, 1923.

56. "Chain of Fact Draws Tighter around Danner," local newspaper (unknown title) (Bozeman, MT) October 1923.

Chapter 6

57. Court transcript, Danner Affidavit, page 40. Gallatin Historical Society.

58. "Defense Finds Itself Unable to Shake Testimony of Main Witness," *Bozeman Courier*, October 24, 1923.

59. Court transcript, Iva Danner Testimony, page 92.

60. "Jury Finds Seth Orrin Danner Guilty of First Degree Murder," *Bozeman Courier*, October 31, 1923.

61. "Sprouse's Dog Returns to Scene of Double Murder," *Bozeman Daily Chronicle*, June 10, 1923.

62. "Defense Finds Itself Unable to Shake Testimony of Main Witness."

63. Ibid.

Chapter 7

64. Court transcript, Iva Danner Testimony, page 155.
65. Ibid., page 176.
66. "Sprouse Visits Danner's Home in Three Forks," *Bozeman Daily Chronicle*, July 8, 1923.
67. "Danner Will Not Go on Stand in His Own Behalf," *Bozeman Daily Chronicle*, October 26, 1923.
68. Court transcript, Testimony of J.E. Overholser, Gallatin Historical Society.
69. "Defense Finds Itself Unable to Shake Testimony of Main Witness."

Chapter 8

70. Court transcript, Instructions to the Jury. Gallatin Historical Society.
71. Court transcript, Danner Affidavit, page 254, September 6, 1923.
72. Ibid., 264.
73. Ibid., 265.
74. Ibid., 267.
75. Ibid.
76. Ibid.
77. Ibid., 269.
78. Ibid.
79. Ibid., 281.
80. Ibid.
81. Ibid.
82. Ibid., 283.
83. Ibid., 291.
84. Ibid., 291. Gallatin Historical Society.
85. Court transcript, Danner Affidavit, page 298, September 6, 1923.
86. "Danner Will Not Go on Stand in His Own Behalf," *Bozeman Daily Chronicle*, October 26, 1923.
87. Court transcript, Florence Danner Testimony, page 310.
88. "Danner Will Not Go on Stand in His Own Behalf."
89. Court transcript, Danner Affidavit, pages 341–42.
90. "Danner's Punishment," local newspaper (title unknown) (Bozeman, MT), October 27, 1923.
91. Ibid.
92. Ibid.
93. Ibid.

94. Ibid.

95. Ibid.

96. "Jury Finds Seth Orrin Danner Guilty of First Degree Murder."

97. Court transcript, *State of Montana vs Seth Orrin Danner*, verdict, page 353.

Chapter 9

98. "Danner Is Peeved When Disturbed to Listen to Verdict," local newspaper (title unknown) (Bozeman, MT), October 28, 1923.

99. "Court Imposes Death Sentence on S.O. Danner," local newspaper (Bozeman, MT), October 1923.

100. Ibid.

101. "Danner Is Peeved When Disturbed to Listen to Verdict," local newspaper (title unknown) (Bozeman, MT), October 28, 1923.

102. Ibid.

103. Ibid.

104. "Jury Finds Seth Orrin Danner Guilty of First Degree Murder."

105. "Danner Sleeping and Eating Well," local paper (title unknown), 1923.

106. "Jury Finds Seth Orrin Danner Guilty of First Degree Murder."

107. "Total Cost of Danner Murder Trial, $1581.33," local paper (title unknown) (Bozeman, MT), October 1923.

108. "Danner in Good Spirits Since Strain of Trial," local paper (title unknown) (Bozeman, MT), October 1923.

109. "Mrs. Iva Danner Weds 'Baker Jim'," *Bozeman Courier*, November 28, 1923.

110. "Danner Pleased with Marriage of Former Wife," *Bozeman Daily Chronicle*, November 1923.

111. Ibid.

112. "Danner Hearing Is Set for Saturday," *Bozeman Courier*, December 12, 1923.

113. "Jurors Swear Danner Given Unbiased Trial," local paper (title unknown) (Bozeman, MT) 1923.

114. "Danner to Hang Friday, Jan. 11 Court Decides," local paper (title unknown) (Bozeman, MT) 1923.

115. "Danner Still Hopeful," *Bozeman Courier*, January 2, 1924.

116. "Danner Seems to Be Losing Nerve," *Bozeman Courier*, January 4, 1924.

117. Ibid.

118. "Danner Insists He's Innocent and Won't Hang," local paper (Bozeman, MT), January 1924.

119. "Danner Still Hopeful."

120. "Filing of Appeal to Supreme Court Halts Plans for Danner's Execution," *Bozeman Courier*, January 16, 1924.

Chapter 10

121. "Filing of Appeal to Supreme Court Halts Plans for Danner's Execution," *Bozeman Courier*, January 16, 1924.

122. "Death Watch Over Danner Day and Night," *Bozeman Daily Chronicle*, December 1923.

123. "Danner's Fate to Be Decided in Short Time," local paper (Bozeman, MT) 1924.

124. "Danner Morose and Silent as He Reads Paper," local paper (title unknown) (Bozeman, MT), May, 28, 1924.

125. "Danner Shows No Signs of Breaking Down," *Bozeman Daily Chronicle*, July 10, 1924.

126. "Slayer's Wife Tells Why She Revealed Crime," *Bozeman Daily Chronicle*, June 16, 1923.

127. "Accused Slayer Still Maintains He Is Innocent," *Bozeman Daily Chronicle*, July 29, 1923.

128. Ibid.

129. Ibid.

130. "Danner Nerve Cracks Before Lady Visitor." *Bozeman Daily Chronicle*, August 12, 1923.

131. "Jury Finds Seth Orrin Danner Guilty of First Degree Murder."

132. "Danner Nerve Cracks Before Lady Visitor."

133. Franklin O. Smith, letter to Governor Dixon, November 27, 1923. Montana Governor's Papers, MC35, Box 255, Folder 15, Montana Historical Society.

134. "Defense Finds Itself Unable to Shake Testimony of Main Witness."

Chapter 11

135. "Danner Writes Letter Which Accuses Wife," local paper (Bozeman, MT), December 1923.

136. Moody, Mabel. Letter to Governor Dixon. January 2, 1924. Montana Governor's Papers, MC35, Box 255, Folder 15, Montana Historical Society.

137. "Danner's Sister is Here on Visit," *Bozeman Courier*, February 6, 1924.

138. Mabel Moody, letter to Governor Dixon. July 1, 1924. Montana Governor's Papers, MC35, Box 255, Folder 15, Montana Historical Society.

139. Lucy Marlow, letter to Governor Dixon. July 8, 1924. Montana Governor's Papers, MC35, Box 255, Folder 15, Montana Historical Society.

140. King, Mrs. Lula B. Letter to Governor Dixon. December 17, 1923. Montana Governor's Papers, MC35, Box 255, Folder 15, Montana Historical Society.

141. Dixon, Governor. Letter to Mrs. Lula B. King. December 24, 1923. Montana Governor's Papers, MC35, Box 255, Folder 15, Montana Historical Society.

142. King, Mrs. Lula B. Letter to Governor Dixon. January 2, 1924. Montana Governor's Papers, MC35, Box 255, Folder 15, Montana Historical Society.

143. Ibid.

144. Secretary, Governor Dixon. Letter to Mrs. Lula B. King. 1924. Montana Governor's Papers, MC35, Box 255, Folder 15, Montana Historical Society.

145. King, Mrs. Lula B. Letter to Governor Dixon. July 11, 1924. Montana Governor's Papers, MC35, Box 255, Folder 15, Montana Historical Society.

146. Ibid.

147. Ibid.

148. Dixon, Governor. Letter to Mrs. Lula B. King. July 14, 1924. Montana Governor's Papers, MC35, Box 255, Folder 15, Montana Historical Society.

149. Betz, Mrs. John. Letter to Governor Dixon. June 10, 1924. Montana Governor's Papers, MC35, Box 255, Folder 15, Montana Historical Society.

150. Dixon, Governor. Letter to Mrs. John Betz. June 12, 1924. Montana Governor's Papers, MC35, Box 255, Folder 15, Montana Historical Society.

151. Lott, Mignor Quaw. Letter to Governor Dixon. July 10, 1924. Montana Governor's Papers, MC35, Box 255, Folder 15, Montana Historical Society.

Chapter 12

152. "Danner Morose and Silent as He Reads Paper," local paper (title unknown) (Bozeman, MT), May 28, 1924.

153. "Danner's Fate Is Sealed by Court," *Bozeman Courier*, June 11, 1924.

154. "Friday, July 18 Execution Date Fixed by Court," *Bozeman Daily Chronicle*, July 17, 1924.

155. "Danner Shows No Signs of Breaking Down."

156. "Friday, July 18 Execution Date Fixed by Court."

157. "Seth Orrin Danner to Die Here Friday by Hanging in Jail." *Bozeman Courier*, July 16, 1924.

158. "Danner Ready and Anxious for the End," *Bozeman Daily Chronicle*, July 17, 1924.

159. Ibid.

Chapter 13

160. "Hangman's Noose Claims Danner for Murder of Mrs. John Sprouse," *Bozeman Courier*, July 23, 1924.

161. Ibid.

162. "Friday, July 18 Execution Date Fixed by Court," *Bozeman Daily Chronicle*, July 17, 1924.

163. "Hangman's Noose Claims Danner for Murder of Mrs. John Sprouse."

164. Ibid.

165. Ibid.

166. Ibid.

167. "Danner's Last Speech Looked Like Admission," *Bozeman Daily Chronicle*, July 24, 1924.

168. "Hangman's Noose Claims Danner for Murder of Mrs. John Sprouse."

169. "Danner's Last Speech Looked Like Admission."

170. "Hangman's Noose Claims Danner for Murder of Mrs. John Sprouse."

Chapter 14

171. "Kills Himself in County Jail." *Bozeman Daily Chronicle*, July 24, 1924.

172. "Hangman's Noose Claims Danner for Murder of Mrs. John Sprouse."

173. "Kills Himself in County Jail." *Bozeman Daily Chronicle*, July 24, 1924.

174. Ibid.

175. "Danner to Hang Friday, Jan. 11 Court Decides," local paper (title unknown) (Bozeman, MT), 1923.

176. Joe Stephens, personal communication, September 13, 2019.

177. Ibid.

178. "Hangman's Noose Claims Danner for Murder of Mrs. John Sprouse."

179. Notes from a phone conversation with Danner relative, 1991. Gallatin Historical Society.

180. Judge Law, Court's Response to Peterson.

181. Merrill Burlingame, interview with Frank Seitz. Gallatin Historical Society.

182. Dana Law, personal communication, July 26, 2019.

183. Atwater, "Murders on the Yellowstone Trail."

INDEX

ABOUT THE AUTHOR

Kelly Hartman was raised in Silver Gate, Montana, attending kindergarten through eighth grade at the one-room schoolhouse in Cooke City. She received her AA in art at Northwest Community College in Powell, Wyoming, and her BFA in painting from Western Oregon University in Monmouth, Oregon. She started her museum career as the director of the Cooke City Montana Museum during its opening year. In 2016, she began work as the curator of the Gallatin History Museum in Bozeman, Montana. The museum is housed in the old county jail, where the topic of this book, Seth Danner, paid his sentence on the gallows. Her first book with The History Press was published in the summer of 2019, *A Brief History of Cooke City*.

Visit us at
www.historypress.com